Past Poets
- Future Voices

2010 Poetry Competition for 11-18 year-olds

Staffordshire &
The West Midlands

Allison Jones

First published in Great Britain in 2010 by

Young**Writers**

Remus House
Coltsfoot Drive
Peterborough
PE2 9JX
Telephone: 01733 890066
Website: www.youngwriters.co.uk

Foreword

Young Writers was established in order to promote creativity and a love of reading and writing in children and young adults. We believe that by offering them a chance to see their own work in print, their confidence will grow and they will be encouraged to become the poets of tomorrow.

Our latest competition 'Past Poets - Future Voices' was specifically designed as a showcase for secondary school pupils, giving them a platform with which to express their ideas, aspirations and passions. In order to expand their skills, entrants were encouraged to use different forms, styles and techniques.

Selecting the poems for publication was a difficult yet rewarding task and we are proud to present the resulting anthology. We hope you agree that this collection is an excellent insight into the voices of the future.

Contents

Chesterton Community Sports College, Chesterton

St Dominic's School, Brewood

St Joseph's College, Stoke-on-Trent

Windsor Park Middle School, Uttoxeter

Wood Green High School, Wednesbury

Jarrad Lambie (13 178
Waseelah Smedley (13) 179
Molly Ashfield-Hayes (13)............... 180
Sharnpreet Kaur Cheema (12) 181
Ahmed Hans (13) 182
Nicky Cavell (12) 183
David Young (13).............................. 183
Josh Southall (13)............................ 184
Leanne Stanfield (13) 184

The Poems

Red, White And Blue

Tears as the national anthem bellows
Across the United ground .
The thoughts of pride rippling through my veins.
This is our country!
Together we make it!
As I enter the shopping centre
The clatter of feet remind me
Of a military snare drum beating away.
Those damn advertisements enriching my thoughts.
Online banking.
Home sweet home.
The kettle whistling away.
Pack of biscuits in my hand
Crunching the wrapper.
Oh I forgot to mention,
What's on down the pub.
The match of course!
Coming home down the road
Signing, 'Oi, oh Wolverhampton town!'
My pals supporting me all the way.

Conor Welch (15)
Bishop Milner School, Dudley

My England

Happy England,
We have a Queen on the throne
I feel all breezes that are blown,
We are known for our weather
So down and glum
But it's our proud English people
Who make our days so happy and bright.

Tea and biscuits, what a wonderful delight
Also known for our fish and chips
That taste so heavenly light.
We are apparently posh, yes posh indeed!
This is what my England means to me.

English, Indian, foreign or more
Britain is a known country to all
All over the country,
From north to south and east to west
England is known to be different,
That's definitely sure!

Liz Palmer (15)
Bishop Milner School, Dudley

Untitled

Tea and biscuits is what we adore
Our population grows more and more
We have very strict laws.

Our men go out to war
Being proud of who they are fighting for
Although more of them die, more and more.

Fish and chips with a pint to hand
But all the rubbish polluting our land
All the litterbugs should be banned.

We Brits are proud of our red, white and blue
Together blend a brand new community.

Kirsty Dupree (15)
Bishop Milner School, Dudley

The Picture

This is the picture
That has kept
Me company
Over the past
Four years.
The one that has
Kept me
Safe and calm.
The one that's kept me happy.

You may be wondering
Who this person is
In the picture.
Well, that is my dad.
We didn't expect
Him to go so soon.
But when I
Have that
Picture, I'm OK.

Whitney Bryan (11)
Bristnall Hall Technology College, Oldbury

3

My Dog

This is the dog
That is always happy.
That learnt what a cat is.
That made new friends
And enemies too.
That makes anyone happy
Even when they are down.
That runs into trees
And gates and walls
And doesn't feel a thing.
That I love to bits.

This is not the dog
That will bite
That no one will remember.
That would hurt anything moving
Or not moving.
That will forget people.
That will run away.
That will stop loving me.
But she is loved by everyone
For her craziness.

Leanne Bragg (11)
Bristnall Hall Technology College, Oldbury

My Purple Gloves

My purple gloves
The gloves I wore
When I was just three
In the wintery cold days
When I would play in the snow.

My gloves that I left on my nursery wall
And ran back to get them.
But now they only fit half of my hand
But will keep my thoughts warm forever!

Symrun Sanghera (11)
Bristnall Hall Technology College, Oldbury

4

My Beautiful Bike!

This is the bike
That my nan bought me years ago.
This bike was pink and girly
With lots of lovely flowers.
It had bright colours.
It had a ringing bell,
It had purple pedals,
It had plain white wheels.

When I was young
This beautiful bike
Took me on journeys
Like no other bike in the world.
We rode up and down the peaceful hills
And places we've never even before.

But now my beautiful bike
Is no longer beautiful.
It's in a dusty shed
Rotting away.
How I miss my beautiful bike!

Rikita Bains (12)
Bristnall Hall Technology College, Oldbury

My Bike

This is the bike I looked at for ages,
It wasn't exactly ages but it felt like it.
The bike my grandad bought me as soon as I told him I liked it.
The bike my cousins helped me to ride.
The bike I rode on my grandad's road.
The bike that took me to the park.
The bike that I said I would ride the Birmingham canals.
The bike that took me everywhere.
The bike I will never throw away.
The bike that I will never forget.
The bike that holds all my memories.

Amrit Bath (11)
Bristnall Hall Technology College, Oldbury

5

My Blanket

This is the blanket
That I loved.
This is the blanket
That comforted me.
This is the blanket
That absorbed my tears.
This is the blanket
That I never left alone.
I loved this blanket until it was gone.
Eventually my sister found it,
My sister kept warm with this blanket.
My sister slept with this blanket
But this blanket slowly gained holes and turned colourless
So my sister gave this blanket to my nan.
My nan cherished this blanket until she passed away.
After my nan had passed, I took the blanket back,
I put the blanket somewhere safe.
To his day the blanket is still under my bed,
I look at it sometimes and remember what it's been through.

Jack Eggington (12)
Bristnall Hall Technology College, Oldbury

My Doll

This is the doll
I held and hugged
Every day and everywhere
I wouldn't be seen without her.

This is the doll
That was held by the arm
It has one eye and no left leg
It has been with me through thick and thin
This is the doll my mum bought me.

Now I'm too old to be playing with her
She happily sits in a box underneath my bed.

Katie Best (11)
Bristnall Hall Technology College, Oldbury

6

The Boots

These are the boots
The boots I've scored in
The boots I've dazzled defenders in
The boots I've won, lost and drawn in
These are the boots
Which I have won trophies in
Boots I've tackled and slid in
The boots I've felt proud in
And have helped me through the good and bad times
These are the boots
I've kept
In my room
To remind me
Remind me of the good times
And not bad
These are the boots
With all my memories.

Jack Floyd (12)
Bristnall Hall Technology College, Oldbury

My First Pair Of Shoes

These are the shoes
I took my first steps in.
When I played in the garden
Or even in the park
These are the shoes
I would put on a few years ago.

But now they are
Under the bed
And now they are
Waiting to be used,
But now they are too small for me.
All they do now
Is hold memories.

Ryan Dwyer (11)
Bristnall Hall Technology College, Oldbury

7

The Cat

This is the cat
I used to play with,
Tell secrets and feed.
It's the cat I used
To call when it's dinner time.
It's the cat I made toys
For when he was bored.
It's the cat
I used to hold when he was scared.
It's the cat I stroked
Before bedtime.
It's the cat I love!
Now he's gone
Away forever.
But I will remember,
I loved him.

Karolina Budaite (11)
Bristnall Hall Technology College, Oldbury

Jingling Teddy

I had a teddy at the end of my cot
All red, white and blue.
It had a bell on its foot
Plus jam on its only ear.

How dearly I did love it,
I played with it all day through.
It jingled while I moved it
Through the whole year.

When I felt sleepy
I always dreamt of the day ahead.
But I soon had my own bed and room,
My mom threw it away.
I sat there wishing
Just to see it one more day.

Nicole Pointon (11)
Bristnall Hall Technology College, Oldbury

8

I Love You All My Life

I love you all my life, now and forever
I will always love you and whatever trials I will come closer
I will always be faithful and true to you
You have given me hope, made me stronger in times when I am
blue.

The hope which I thought was really hard to find
Just came along the way just at the right time
The time in which no more tears left to cry
Your hugs of comfort ease my pain now there's no need to cry.

I am amazed of how you filled my heart with so much love
You treat me like a princess, so glad how you raise me up above
You have been pouring out so much love from your heart my dear
And all my life I will serve and love you
I will love you all my life now and forever.

Ryan Colledge (13)
Bristnall Hall Technology College, Oldbury

Stars Shine No Brighter Than Your Eyes

Stars shine no brighter than your eyes
Sparkling in summer's evening skies.
Your smile lights up my day
The sun lights my day less, no matter what's to say.
You are more amazing than a swallow's first flights
Even the moon on a cold winter's night.
Your lips are as perfect as a freshly baked cake
More than a spring flower first awakes.
Your embrace is as warm as the sunshine in spring
I would love you forever, more than anything.
I will love you forever and forever will be
More meaningful than anything or nothing to me.
As Shakespeare once said, 'Love can't be thy name'
For if you were anything else, my love for you is the same.

Phoebe Hinton-Sheley (13)
Bristnall Hall Technology College, Oldbury

9

Jelly Beans

As I walk down the road
You sit on the shelf in the shop
There was always a flavour I wouldn't eat, toad
But cola always tasted the best.
Sometimes they tasted lovely
But sometimes they tasted nasty.
I would always choose you over jubbly
Even if it was jelly bean flavour.
The times you weren't in the shop
I could cry all day.
I also loved the ones that went pop!
The explosion was amazing.
I hope you never run out
Otherwise I will cry and shout!

Jonathan Davies (12)
Bristnall Hall Technology College, Oldbury

Home Is Where My Heart Lies

Home is where my heart lies
This has to be said
It may not be my dream house
With a four-poster bed.
It may not hold the key to all of my wishes
It may not have a Garden of Eden filled with one hundred fishes
But the atmosphere is brilliant, the company is great
It has sentimental values that I just can't contemplate.
I feel like I am in a bubble
Isolated from the rest of the world.
My home is where my heart lies
This is true
My home is where my heart lies
What about you?

Katie McCarron (12)
Bristnall Hall Technology College, Oldbury

My First Bike

Leaping on my bike
I ride through the wind
Pretending I am in a race
I am the one who always wins
I make it look all shiny
I clean it with a cloth
I love my bike so much
I will never let it go

But I am too old for it now
It is too small
I have a new bike now
Bigger and better than before
But I will always love my first bike.

Isobel Stokes (11)
Bristnall Hall Technology College, Oldbury

My Bike

This is the bike
I first rode on.
The bike took me on adventures
Down the streets,
In the parks.
The bike that got me muddy
Whenever I went out.

But now it is locked up
Away in the shed,
Rotting away
Without any thought.
I grew up with this bike
But it is going forever.

Taiyab Bashir (12)
Bristnall Hall Technology College, Oldbury

Teddy Bear

Even though you have gone
You're still in my heart.
You were given to me by my mom
We'll never be apart.

You were pink and blue
You always had a smiley face.
Even when you had the flu
You always sent me to a happy place.

When I took you to school
You were the only one there.
You looked so cool
You were the best teddy bear.

Amber Marshall (12)
Bristnall Hall Technology College, Oldbury

Pie

I love pie filled with mince
Or apples and juices sprinkled with sugar.
I've loved pie ever since I was given one from my mother.
But now my pie is gone and I didn't eat any pie.
I think it was him, the one called Ron,
Only crumbs on his plate, oh why, oh why?
Why would he eat the pie I made?
It clearly was mine!
Why do my pies always fade?
Maybe it is time.
So now I leave this world so cold
Because a world without pie is not a livable world.

Aiden Ashton (13)
Bristnall Hall Technology College, Oldbury

The Teddy Bear

This is the teddy bear
I took everywhere.
When I went to Nan's,
In the garden,
On holiday,
When Dad got a new car,
When I stayed at my auntie's.
This is the teddy bear
I keep in my room
On the end of my bed.

Charlotte Hill (11)
Bristnall Hall Technology College, Oldbury

The Painting

This is the painting I did in Reception.
The painting that helped me learn my colours.
This is the painting that made me feel proud.
The painting that my mum framed.
This is the painting that I used to love,
The painting that always cheers me up.
Now the painting doesn't look so good,
All the colours are faded.
But even though it is no longer nice,
It will be treasured forever.

Lauren Grove (12)
Bristnall Hall Technology College, Oldbury

The Boots

The boots that I wear are ones that keep me warm.
The boots that I wear are ones that I mount my horses with.
When it rains they keep my feet dry.
I polish them like they are a treasure in a box.
They glimmer in the sunlight like a star.
When I walk they make my favourite noise
That gives me a warming feeling inside.
When I grow out of them they will always keep
The memories that I've had in them.
The boots that I wore I will love for evermore.

Yazmin Millward (12)
Bristnall Hall Technology College, Oldbury

My Book

My book
My book, my secret book,
The book that holds and shares my pain and tears.
The book that holds and shares my happiness and love, that holds my secrets.
This book I feel is like a friend that I can share anything with,
Like my hopes and wishes and I keep it safe in my room where no one can find it.

Leia Martin (12)
Bristnall Hall Technology College, Oldbury

I Still Believe . . .

Being locked in cold tiny spaces
Surrounded by many other sad faces
Hardly have any clothes on
Not knowing where my parents have gone
Working all day in the cold
Catching a cold that will not go.
I still believe . . .
Why am I in this camp?
Easy to say, but is hard to understand.

Soldiers surveying every act we're doing
Their eyes fix on us as we're moving.
Wondering when my parents will come
And the realising after so long, they've gone.
That's it; they've gone, gone forever.
Tears sprint out my eyes just like rainfall
I know no more because I am small.

I'm so weak that I can't work anymore
Why are they making us do this work?
I ask myself.
I want an answer but I can't find it
Thinking back to what I had, the love, hope, peace
But in my heart . . . I still believe in peace.
A peace that will not end,
A peace that will flow like waterfall,
A peace that is not surrounded with hate
But a peace that only means one thing.
A peace that leads to freedom, fresh start, new life and hope, love,
care.
I still believe.

Andreas Makosso (11)
Cardinal Wiseman School & Language College, Coventry

Me

Can I see what is around me?
All I see is me.
Not too tall, not too short, just me.
What could be more important to me?
Can you see how important I am to me?
Will you understand me?

My mum understands me,
She will always love me.
She never asks too much of me.
She always makes time for me, not judging me.
She will always be with me.

When it is just me all I can see is me.
When there is no one to talk to only me
What could I say to me?
What a fool, I am talking to me
I don't like it when it is just me
I like my friends all around me
Being happy, just like me.

Biagio Gallo (12)
Cardinal Wiseman School & Language College, Coventry

In The Night

As the shining moon lights up the city
All homes are dark.
Tumbling stones fall against the seashore
When night winds roar moonlight shines along the gentle seashore.
The blacked out trees dance along the open sea.
Stars twinkle in the colourful sky.
Moon shines like a crystal ball floating in the sky.
Clouds look like cotton wool balls smothered in pitch-black paint.
All is calm, sea sleeping stars twinkle,
Moon smiles looking down upon us,
So quiet, no sound, no movement, all is fast asleep,
Safe and sound.

Isaac Alleyne (12)
Cardinal Wiseman School & Language College, Coventry

Fixed To The Spot

The earthquake sent shivers down my spine
But I was fixed to the spot
The ground was shaking violently
But I was fixed to the spot
The dark cloud closed in on me
But I was fixed to the spot
The lightning imprisoned me
But I was fixed to the spot
The rain spat at me
But I was fixed to the spot
Thunder bellowed
But I was fixed to the spot
I chose to run . . . too late . . .

Tunde Salawu (12)
Cardinal Wiseman School & Language College, Coventry

Summertime

Now at last, summer's finally here
All you can see is dads drinking beer.
All the small children shout
That all they want is the pool out!

Now that the weather is so hot
We need the sunscreen, not just a little, we need a lot!
Oh when out comes the sun
That's when we really have fun!

Grilled chicken on the barbecue
Along came the flies that we must shoo.
As the grass turns from green to yellow
'Move out the way,' we hear Dad bellow.

Chewing on the pieces of melon makes us smile
But only for a little short while.
For here now comes down the rain
Another bad summer, here we go again!

Megan Whitehouse (11)
Chasetown Specialist Sports College, Chasetown

17

As The Snow Falls

As the snow falls
The school calls
To let out a shout
That school's out
I slide on the ice
As I throw a snowball, nice.

When school does close
I have cold toes
For playing out all day
As I walk away
I get hit on the head
So I go to bed.

The next morning
Is so boring
As I walk to school
It is not cool
As people moan
And groan.

Then comes lunch
We all have a munch
As the snowballs fly
People start to cry
After lunch we have lessons
And go to sessions.

When I get home
We go to the snow dome
As we have a blast
It doesn't really last
As the day ends
There are no more trends.

As the snow goes
I no longer have cold toes
As the sun comes out
People shout
Now some people are glad
Whereas others are sad.

As the snow falls
The school calls.

Elisha Hardwick (13)
Chasetown Specialist Sports College, Chasetown

Our World

Our world is a happy place,
Our world filled with different race.
In countries filled with poverty and kill,
Religions at war, in fields, on hill.
Green oceans, skies of blue,
Cities and towns, stuck together like glue.

Living in a place where you don't have a clue,
People walking around chanting, how do you do?
Running to the taxis and underground tubes,
Filling our planet with gasses and fumes.
Melting the Arctic, heating the Earth,
What about the polar bears, doesn't it hurt?

Teenagers giving birth, women dying of cancer,
People's lives lost, is it really the answer?
Sit and think about what can be done,
Can we stop those teenagers from carrying a gun?
Places to go, people to see,
Living our life being nothing, just me.
My world filled with people,
Families and friends, houses and cars
In a world so big, with everyone so far.

Evie Hinks (12)
Chasetown Specialist Sports College, Chasetown

19

Haiti Earthquake Disaster Poem

Thousands of people dead
Children's faces covered in red.

The country has changed forever
No matter how much we endeavour.

No words can describe the pain
It hits people like a speeding train.

So much suffering and blood
And all people can see is thick slushy mud.

It will be there forever and ever
Will never go away, never.

People are scarred for life
Every man and his wife.

Some did not live to tell the tale
They struggled to live but ended in fail.

The ground shook like never before
They thought it ended but it happened even more.

It measured high on the Richter Scale
And made millions of faces turn pale.

Children killed within seconds
The voice of death beckons.

Houses came tumbling down
Destroying hundreds of people and their town.

The disaster is all over the news
That Haiti will be left with a bruise.

Charities are doing all they can
But they just need a Superman.

So please help the Haiti Foundation
By giving your kind donations.

Brad Littler (14)
Chasetown Specialist Sports College, Chasetown

A Walk In The Dark

'Twas a cold winter's night
As we walked across the land
With the moon shining bright
We walked hand in hand

There was nothing to see and nowhere to go
As we stumbled and tumbled through trees and so
We continued to follow what we knew best
Our own intuition being put to the test

It was dark and cold and there was nowhere to rest
As we stumbled and tumbled we came across an old oak chest
What was in the old box we just didn't care
All that we wanted was to get out of there.

What had we found and where were we
And what would happen to us three
In the middle of nowhere with no one around?
All alone, not a single sound.

Running together as fast as we could
Through that very dark and uninviting wood
Our breathing was rapid and our hearts racing hard
Each of us wanting to be back in our own yards.

And finally we saw a shining white light
As we trekked through the trees on that cold dark night
With each us deciding to run as fast as we can
As we finally saw a small white van

In the middle of the night with nowhere to go
We had found our way out on to the road
From the depth of the trees in the middle of nowhere
We had finally someone who cared

To take us home is where we wanted to be
All of us together, finally free.

Emma Lynam (13)
Chasetown Specialist Sports College, Chasetown

21

Change

Green as grass should forever be;
The field - once it glowed bright.
Now the green - life can never see;
Blacks and browns block the light.

Flowers dance in a pleasant breeze;
Their colours smile at me.
Tall towers now my child sees;
On the grave of a tree.

These changes and my old, good life;
Their presence is a crime.
My small children will live in strife;
Robbed of a better time.

Once I saw vast, green open plains;
Now them I cannot reach.
Urban monsters, terrible cranes;
Now this is all we teach.

I remember greens, pinks and blue;
These things were all around.
Now it appears - to my rue;
These things cannot be found.

Never will you see a bluebell;
Or a beautiful rose.
This cold, new life is a true hell;
I feel my life is froze.

Now all there is, is blocks of stone;
I don't know where to go.
I found a tall, old pine tree - lone;
The last of an old row.

I called to its mind, I looked behind;
To when we both were better.

Joshua Baggott (13)
Chasetown Specialist Sports College, Chasetown

Life On Earth

In the storm turning the thoughts
Watching extensively into the cloud bank
Silenced speeches floating effortlessly
The rush and pound of the city below
Whistling wind of many a blow.

In the north a clouded temple
To the east a weeping chorus
To the south a song of time
To the west a mile to stride.

In the centre stands alone
A moaning tree
A tree that time has tested
A radiant glow
With a pool to each side
History it doth show.

A descending mist
Of which a strike of sunlight does appear
Cascading light is erased
From the earth shadows dance.

Too still in a falling stance
A crumbling Earth
Round flourishing plants.

As the gazing moon
Watches with an eager eye
To soothe the shadow
That doth cry.

A flash of light
Turns the dark
A new day
Until the light doth fade away.

Emily Kent (14)
Chasetown Specialist Sports College, Chasetown

When I . . .

When I see the glowing golden sun
It makes me smile and feel warm inside.
When I see the shining blue sky
It makes me think about the salty blue sea.

When I smell the tea cooking at night
It makes me think about all the poor and ill people.
When I hear children playing happily
It makes my heart feel content.

When I taste the luscious sweets
It makes my mouth water and want more treats.
When I touch a baby's skin
It's smooth and soft like velvet.

When I find the one I love
They always cause heartache and pain.
When I get home to family and friends
We sit and talk about the day we've had.

When I describe my personality
I sometimes use my imagination.
When I describe my home
I talk about my mom, sister and pets.

When I describe myself
I say I'm as smiley as a hyena.
When I go out with my friends
I have a laugh and a joke.

When I finally think I've found the one I love
They end up breaking my heart.
When I go on holiday
I enjoy the atmosphere around me.
That's my life!

Aimee Charlotte Jukes (13)
Chasetown Specialist Sports College, Chasetown

Sport

Rugby is swell
But it really makes you smell.
You really want a shower
The taste of power is really sour.

Football is a blow
And it really makes you go.
It's the end of the half,
The fans wave their scarf.

Golf is calm,
Playing by the palm.
Get the ball in the bunker
All the players wear their jumper.

Basketball is so much fun
The speed is like a bullet from a gun.
The players do an impressive loop
When they shoot through the hoop.

Hockey is cool
But defence is a drool.
Hit the puck in the net
Soon after you will sweat.

Tennis is so fast
One wrong move you're in a cast.
Hit the ball with the racket
When it comes back just smack it.

Keep the ball away from the wicket
That's how you play cricket.
Throw the ball past the batter
Hit the sticks, the crowd clatter.

James Cowell (11)
Chasetown Specialist Sports College, Chasetown

Space

The sun roars in the sky
In the universe way up high
It glistens and shimmers as planets spin past
Then the moon blocks its rays in the universe vast

The moon spinning uncontrollably fast
Blocking the light as it crosses its path
Turning the planet into darkness below
Leaving the world with nothing to show

The world is in orbit around the sun
Following its leader since time has begun
Half of the countries now still and silent
Yet the other half are buzzing and violent

In one of these countries now quiet and peaceful
Lies many people positive and wishful
Who are losing energy like a wind-up toy
Waiting for another day to share their joy

In this country there lies a town
With mixed emotions, smiles and frowns
The streets are empty but their hearts are full
Not a single thing to them seems dull

In this town there is a street
And if you go there you will meet
Diverse people from every race
Yet not one of them feels out of place

On this street there lies a house
With people there dreaming about
The universe above them light years away
Yet there they like and here they stay.

Amy Wilson (13)
Chasetown Specialist Sports College, Chasetown

In My Mind

Today, tomorrow, in my mind I see,
Kids, birds, life flashing past me.
Some people say tomorrow never comes
I just listen to the bird that hums.

Bright colours in my mind I see
Happy, laughter, love, happy with glee.
The loud sound that whizzes past
The sweet lonely sound, wishing it would last.
Sometimes I wish I could live forever
Happy and sad times wishing I could be clever.
So much to think about, so much to do,
Such lovely colours like pink and blue.
Days go by so quick yet so slow
Such lovely feelings wishing they would never go.
In my mind I see
Careers, dreams, things I would love to be.
Life flashes by like you're reading a book
You never know when your life might be took.
Make the most of the things you want to do
The rest is up to you.
The beautiful nature and sights to see
The wonderful world around you and me.
We are so lucky even to this day
Make the most of life I say.

Today, tomorrow in my mind I see
Kids, birds, life flashing past me.
Some people say tomorrow never comes
I just listen to the bird that hums.

Melanie Moore (13)
Chasetown Specialist Sports College, Chasetown

Sherry

Standing there in a field
A dark chestnut stands
Motionless in beauty.

The wind whirls around her
But yet she still stands still
Her red coat must keep her warm
Through this winter chill.

She thuds her hoof impatiently
Loud enough to hear
Her head turns towards me
I feel no dread or fear.

Then, the wind stops
Her mane lays flat to my sight
And in the distance the sun rises
Turning her to light.

She turns to the sun
Rearing up to the sky
All of the darkness gone from her
Except from her circular eye.

The smell of the grass from the fields
Spinning around my head softly
But all I can do is stare
As Sherry gallops away
Into the sun's bright rays.

Adele Mabley (13)
Chasetown Specialist Sports College, Chasetown

Me And My Clothes

My shoes sat in my wardrobe
My shoes sat on my feet
They made me feel real comfortable
When walking down the street.

My hat sat on the hat stand
My hat sat on my head
I had it on all day long
Though I had to take it off for bed.

My top was in my wardrobe
My top was on my belly
I wore it for too many days
And made it go all smelly.

My skirt sat on the hanger
My skirt sat round my waist
It was a rather funky item
Which showed I had good taste.

My headband sat in the drawer
My headband sat in my hair
My headband was the colour blonde
So it looked just like real hair.

My clothes sit all about the place
My clothes they sit on me
I wear them in a certain way
And that's what makes me, me!

Sophia Chipman (11)
Chasetown Specialist Sports College, Chasetown

Waiting In The Wings

I stand so straight, so tall, so still,
The reason I'm here? I suppose my will,
Determined and ready, but it's just for fun,
Doesn't matter if you have lost or won.

Emotions raging high and low,
Though my mind is focused on when to go,
But it's hard enough to keep in mind,
That the curtains are there to hide behind.

As the music starts to play,
I realise that this is the time and day,
Then I listen for my cue,
Oh please don't let people boo.

The contrast of the soothing music,
And my violent beating heart.
This doesn't feel like pleasure,
Just an awkward art.

My body relaxes, I start to dance,
More of a lullaby than a prance.
The audience watch expectantly,
I hope they enjoy it as much as me.

As I depart from the stage,
I realise that I have got to an age
Where this is a magical journey,
From the wings right through to the curtsey.

Molly Eve Beardsmore (14)
Chasetown Specialist Sports College, Chasetown

My 30 Yard Dream

I see it coming to me
The crowd's on my back
I feel the adrenaline
As I give it a thwack!

I feel it in the air
The crowd begin to rise
I'm hoping for it to go in
A miss is what I despise.

It's getting closer and closer
I smell victory
As it travels 30 yards
It's really getting to me.

Smash! Into the back of the net
The crowd's on their feet
I knew I saved my team
From a bitter defeat.

I start to celebrate
The whole ground shakes
Stroke of luck or well perfected
It's the whole team that makes.

At the special dinner
I feel the aftermath
I relive that great goal
As the opposition feel my wrath!

Josh Langley (13)
Chasetown Specialist Sports College, Chasetown

The Soldiers Come

The world we knew
It's hard to see
People come
And try not to flee.

They spread courage
Covering fear
Tonight they come
So perfectly clear.

Their uniforms so dull
Their hearts so bright
With determination
To give us some light.

The hospitals overflow
They cannot cope
But the men do not surrender
Not to destroy our hope.

Eventually we will die
Or live to celebrate
But whatever happens
It is our fate.

We need to fight
As hard as we can
To save all mankind
Not just one man.

Hayley Cox (13)
Chasetown Specialist Sports College, Chasetown

What Do You Get At A Football Match?

So, what do you get at a football match?

Fans screaming,
Forward leaning.

A ref who is a pain
Because he keeps stopping the game.

A barmy boss
Making players cross.

People wanting fame,
Trying to make their name.

Players who are cunning
And some good at running.

Pies being eaten
And a team being beaten.

Fans standing in the cold
All ages, from young to old.

Guys at the game
Shouting the best player's name.

Lots more cheering
When the end is nearing

And that's what you get at a football match.

Rebecca Atkins (12)
Chasetown Specialist Sports College, Chasetown

Snowy Monday Morning

It's cold, it's frosty, it is snowing,
It is Monday morning and I need to get going.
I will phone my mate
To tell her I will be late.
Do I walk or do I run?
No I'll slide, it is much more fun!

Paige Russell (11)
Chasetown Specialist Sports College, Chasetown

33

The Unsinkable

In the port the Unsinkable floats
Largest and the boldest of all boats
After a while a boiler's alight
Sailing the Unsinkable out of sight.

Off it goes, far out to sea
Like a great white swimming free.
Faster and faster, Atlantic's in the view
How many icebergs? Only a few.

Cold and dark, moving with stealth
Eating the party food to yourself
Cheer and joy of waving a ticket
Hoping someone won't nick it.

Further and further into the dark
Nowhere to stay and nowhere to park.
Turning away from the route ahead
Can only mean all onboard dead.

So it came to pass the unsinkable sank
Snapping each and every last plank.
Everyone worrying and starting to panic
That's the last time they saw the Titanic.

James Townsend (13)
Chasetown Specialist Sports College, Chasetown

Seasons

Seasons, there are four,
No less, no more.
There is winter which is cold and blue
Also there is spring which is fresh and new.
Autumn has a slight breeze
While summer is chased by bees.
These are the seasons, these are them all
The seasons are the reasons why trees grow tall
And why birds call.

Ellie Birch (12)
Chasetown Specialist Sports College, Chasetown

Forbidden Love

The moon shone down like beams from Heaven
Desire, lust and magic whispered through the wind
A forbidden love
Was forever sinned.

The gates opened and he fell
A fallen angel came to me
His body shattered and broken
A thousand nightmares were all he could see.

As you approached, times stood still,
The moment you saw
How evil you were to me
A frozen thaw began to thaw.

Now we are together, we'll never be apart
If you ripped one of us away
We will always keep the memories
In our hearts they will always stay.

And if you taped our broken hearts back together
They would only spell one word
And that word is the beginning of magic
That word is 'love'.

Charlotte Brindley (12)
Chasetown Specialist Sports College, Chasetown

Sat Upon A Lavatory

I think that I would like to be
Sat upon a lavatory.
The words unfortunately will not come
I think they are stuck up my bum!

A chat, a game, a cup of tea,
None of these write poetry.

I think that I would like to be
Sat upon a lavatory.

Ryan Evans (12)
Chasetown Specialist Sports College, Chasetown

Hoodies

Where are the hoodies?
They're over there!
Where are the hoodies?
There, there, there!

Here they come
All dressed in black.
Here they come
I need to turn my back!

'Help! Help!' I shout in fear.
Now they're so near.
They slow down to meet me
With grins on their faces filled with glee.

'Hello,' a young voice says,
'Don't hurt me.'
He looks so mad
'Why do people think that of me?'

So now I know
They're not all out to get us
And now I know
They are good and not out to hurt us!

Ella Birch (13)
Chasetown Specialist Sports College, Chasetown

Life

Life is like an endless page,
In an eternal book kept by God.
One can only hope to leave a mark on that page.
A mark which will show to those who follow,
What we made of our time
Spent in the moment
That we have here on Earth.
A moment which we call a lifetime.

Siona Bloomer (12)
Chasetown Specialist Sports College, Chasetown

Woodland Wonders

As an eerie mist gradually encroaches over this woodland maze
I watch in awe as the moon boldly shines through the trees.
I rest on a tree stump and in a hypnotic gaze
Overlook this wonderland of mysteries.

The moonlight I see floods the pupil of my eye
The atmosphere here has put me under a spell
Everything seems still at this moment in time
This view is surely once in a lifetime, I can tell.

A wise old owl sweeps over to the tree next to me
Is that a face I see as I cast a glance?
A snake is entwining itself around the trunk of a tree
Am I dreaming or in a trance?

Further and further I wander into the darkness
Jet-black, soulless shadows cast on the ground
I dare not to tread on anything at all
In fear of disturbing any evil that's around!

The clock is ticking and the night grows old
The darkness begins to fade and the owl flaps his wings and flees
I can hear the dawn chorus sing
And the sun rises to cast its golden rays through the trees.

Charlotte Hendley (13)
Chasetown Specialist Sports College, Chasetown

The Beach

The sand sparkles like a ball of light,
People walk on it day and night.
As the sea gets rough and the waves begin to sway
People start to run away.
As the night draws in with a cloudy sky
The moon disappears with a sigh.
As the beach begins to fall asleep
No one can hear a single peep.

Sophie Lyndon-Williams (11)
Chasetown Specialist Sports College, Chasetown

37

Snow

I love it when it starts to snow
I grab my boots and out I go
To watch the flakes fall to the ground
As they land not a sound.

As the snow begins to thicken
I get my sleigh and my steps quicken
To the top of the nearest hill
To come zooming down, oh what a thrill!

I then hurry back to my garden
And as the snow begins to harden
Up and down, I roll the snow
What am I making? I think you know
A snowman with a scarf and hat
Nice and big, round and fat.

I love the snow when it gets deep
And it gets piled up in a heap
Then I can jump in it up to my knees
Hoping that no one sees.

I love it when we have snow
And hate it when it has to go.

Emily Banks (12)
Chasetown Specialist Sports College, Chasetown

Some People

Some people cry,
Some people laugh,
Some people smile,
Some people frown,
But the others,
They swallow their tears,
They hide their frown,
They never let life bring them down.

Lauren Ferguson (13)
Chasetown Specialist Sports College, Chasetown

Can I Have Some Sweets?

When I want some sweets this is how I get them . . .

'Mummy, can I have some sweets?'
'No!'
'Daddy, can I have some sweets?'
'No!'
'Cousin, can I have some sweets?'
'No!'
'Auntie, can I have some sweets?'
'No!'
'Uncle, can I have some sweets?'
'No!'
'Sister, can I have some sweets?'
'No!'
'Brother, can I have some sweets?'
'No!'
'Grandad, can I have some sweets?'
'No!'
'Grandma, can I have some sweets, please?'
'Yes, of course you can dear.'

And that is how I get my sweets!

Stephanie Louise Hancox (12)
Chasetown Specialist Sports College, Chasetown

Football Poem

Jerome is winning races
Villa are going places.
Alex McLeish doesn't mind
While Man U are trying to find
Good players to go and shoot 'n' score
Even though Pompy are starting to bore.
Rafa is yelling and roaring
And Stoke fans are cheering and balling.
Gary Lineker is on 'Match of the Day'
The show tells about football's play.

Lewis Bate (12)
Chasetown Specialist Sports College, Chasetown

My Family

Mum, is where it all begun
The one who gave me life
To support with any of my strife.

She has taught me to be good and kind
To try and help me find
A healthy peace of mind
And to treat others as I like to be.

Dad was there too
He guided me through
Advising me what I need to do
To find my true self.

Grandma, so loving and giving
Generous through and through
Has given me her unconditional love
Like the best grandmothers do.

Grandad the wise one
Always so dependant and fun
He has shared with much laughter and glee
All of these people have helped me become me!

Ryan Poppleton (12)
Chasetown Specialist Sports College, Chasetown

When I Have The Giggles

Intoxicated with giggles
We rock forward and backwards letting out a smile
We don't get the joke but the fun is worthwhile
Now I'm starting to bounce up and down, just like a kangaroo
And so now I'm bursting for the loo!
I'm starting to think what started all of this
I think really hard, while in fits of giggles and my body starts to feel
like thousands of squiggles!
My mother walks in, asks what I'm doing
I answer by saying we're laughing about nothing!

Libbie Davies (11)
Chasetown Specialist Sports College, Chasetown

Comet

The sun soon surrendered, and cowered away,
As a gentle breeze concluded the day.
The moon was restless, as the night approached,
As the time passed, the moon quickly encroached.
Stars rapidly began to conceal the sky,
A pristine scene that brought a tear to my eye.
As I was staring into the great unknown,
Across the sky appeared a gleaming gemstone.
A comet it was, and it brightened the land,
A sight so majestic, a memory so grand.

The colour of silver with a hint of gold,
The colours of power many wished to behold.
Time seemed to halt, to watch the great scene,
As it paraded through the sky like a flying machine.
It started to fade, like it was shrinking in size,
A matter of which, caught me by surprise.
And then it was over. Gone in a flash,
I only had memories, of the comet's quick dash.
I had lost the comet and now the sky was turning black,
From beauty to nothing, the comet's only drawback.

Kimberley Hackett (14)
Chasetown Specialist Sports College, Chasetown

Snow For A Day!

I woke one morning to snow on the ground
Flurries of flakes still fluttering down
Tracks from the cars left behind on the road
Footprints on pavements where people braved the cold
Wrapped up warm with hats, gloves and scarves
Heads to the ground as walking was hard
Children out playing with sledges in hand
Snowball fights and snowmen stand
In the gardens of those who came out to play
As far as they knew it may only last for a day!

Jake Cottrell (11)
Chasetown Specialist Sports College, Chasetown

41

The Circus

Hear, hear, the circus is near.
I'm so happy
I shed a tear.
Hear, hear, the circus is near.

The big top.
Hope the gymnasts don't drop!
Mr Clown
He deserves a crown.
Hear, hear, the circus is near.

The zoo
It may be new.
But the lions of war
They don't half roar!
Hear, hear, the circus is near.

The elephants are round
They would make the world bound.
Their balancing act
They were tightly packed.
Hear, hear, the circus is near.

Luke Wakelin (12)
Chasetown Specialist Sports College, Chasetown

You And Me

A special world for you and me
A special friendship people see
Some people are kind, some not
But maybe they're not all they seem.

A special person just for me
A special life full of glee
With my friends, bubbly and just being me.

Emma Price-Horton (13)
Chasetown Specialist Sports College, Chasetown

The Mysterious Mask

There once was a cave
With a boring mask
Surrounded with lots of grass.

One day it was uncovered
By a girl in the forest
Whose mother was called Doris.

When she went into the cave
There was a massive bang
Then the mask went clang.

The mask was full of colour
With diamonds, pearls and little swirls
It wasn't much duller.

Then the mask started to move
And went further into the cave.

When the cave came to the end
There was a secret door
In there was more . . .
Then that was the end of the mysterious mask.

Danielle Bull (11)
Chasetown Specialist Sports College, Chasetown

I Remember . . . Godzilla!

I remember the time when Godzilla came from under the sea.
I remember people screaming and running around to get away.
I remember the sound of Godzilla's roar and the heat from his fire.
I remember the noise of people's bones being snapped in its mouth.
I remember the size of its footprints forced into the ground.
But now that's all over with and there is no need to worry
But I don't know there might be another nightmare come true.

Jordan Buxton (12)
Chasetown Specialist Sports College, Chasetown

The Willow

The willow's branches twist ferociously
The willow's leaves sway in the depth of night
The willow's roots crack up the ground angrily
The willow's trunk creaks all day from dawn to dusk.

The leaves sway
The branches crackle
The trunk rots
The willow groans
And then summer arrives.
Pleasant children running around the willow
Lovers carving their names on warm nights
Picnics passing under the shade of the willow's leaves
The willow's branches are full of bright birds.
The leaves sparkle
The branches swirl
The life in the willow bustles
The willow smiles
And then the willow sighs for he realises the cold nights will soon be back.

Oliver Clark (13)
Chasetown Specialist Sports College, Chasetown

Dreams And Hopes

D reams are hopes
R easons to be happy
E verything peaceful and great
A world without war
M y dream is to be happy

And

H oping to be cool
O nly to get fooled
P eace on Earth
E veryone would be happy.

Courtney Austin (12)
Chasetown Specialist Sports College, Chasetown

I Can't Write Poems

I was told to write a poem
But I find it hard
I have no ideas good enough
And now I feel like a 'tard'.

So sitting in my English lesson
My pen ready to write,
Yet my brain is a big fat loser
And it might take me all night.

I want to go back to three weeks ago
When I was in sun, sand, sea.
Having fun, not a care in the world
Now I'm at school with Mr B.

So I'll sit and write all this
While I chatter with my best friend,
Even though this poem is pointless
And it needs to end.

Jennifer Peach (14)
Chasetown Specialist Sports College, Chasetown

Losing Life

The flames flicker
As the fire dies.
The different colours
Dance in his eyes.
The heat it's giving
Makes him sweat
As the fire loses life
So does he.
His eyes growing cold
From once filled with glee.
The room loses heat
As the fire dies
The old man's eyes - lifeless.

Emily Smith (12)
Chasetown Specialist Sports College, Chasetown

45

Snow

It's wintertime again
And I wake up not seeing rain.
Instead I see a garden covered in snow,
Just lying there and it will not go.
And still it comes whistling by
In great masses from the sky.

This wintertime we go
Walking round the streets of snow.
While children play all day long
I listen to the robin's song
Then the day draws to an end
As we walk the final bend.

Then I go and put my feet up
Whilst drinking tea from my favourite cup.
And finally it's time to sleep
And hope the snow will keep.

Lucy Harrison (12)
Chasetown Specialist Sports College, Chasetown

Holiday!

I wake up early to catch the plane,
I'm all packed up and ready for Spain!
The flight is just a little boring
And I can even hear some people snoring.
We're nearly there, the runway's in sight,
So glad it's nearly the end of our flight.
Outside it's baking, it's really hot,
The weather at home is long forgot.
The hotel is lovely, it's really posh,
I hope my dad's brought lots of dosh.
I'm having a great time, it's really cool,
I can't wait to see the swimming pool.
We head for the beach with towels and suncream
This holiday no doubt will be a dream.

Hannah Pountney (13)
Chasetown Specialist Sports College, Chasetown

My Football Poem

Football is so much fun
As well I like to run
Every day I play and play
And then say hooray!

When the ball goes in the net
In celebration we all met

When the half time whistle goes
We all have very sore toes

Before you know it, it's the second half
We're all ready with our scarves

People fouling all around
I am listening to the sound

When the final whistle goes
We all shake hands and do a little pose.

Tom Ingleston (11)
Chasetown Specialist Sports College, Chasetown

Tom

My friend Tom was like the stars
But to me he was more than that
He was like the sun, the moon, the Earth and Mars.

When we used to get to school
We used to laugh and joke and act all cool.

Now when I look up he's smiling down at me
His face is full of love and glee.

Then he says, 'Hello' then 'Bye'
Me and my friends say, 'Tom don't go' and start to cry.

When I go to bed at night
I see this lovely shining light.
Tom, every minute I think of you
And I'm pretty sure my friends do too.

Brodie Holland (12)
Chasetown Specialist Sports College, Chasetown

47

Sport

Villa are winning games
Button is taking lanes
Alex McLeish doesn't mind
While Villa are trying to find
Players are going places
Barrichello is winning races
Portsmouth can't win
Young stepped on a pin
Good players can score
And Torres fell to the floor
Villa are world class
I need a VIP pass
Stoke are the loudest team
Milner is shooting with a beam
He is on 'Match of the Day'
He has got good pay.

Nathan Ashford (11)
Chasetown Specialist Sports College, Chasetown

Heaven

As I awoke from my bed
It wasn't to the normal smell of toasted bread.
But to birds tweeting to a marvellous lullaby
And sunbeams glaring down from the sky.

As I strolled towards my door
I realised my feet were no longer on the floor.
And as a bird fluttered around holding my aura
My face turned red with horror.

I ran outside only to find clouds
Little did I know I was wrapped in a shroud.

As I awoke from my bed
I realised I was dead.

This was Heaven.

Jake Bowdler (13)
Chasetown Specialist Sports College, Chasetown

Maths!

Oh no, what's next?
I need to send a text.
It's maths, that's what
Argh, I forgot!
We are probably doing algebra,
Fractions,
Decimals,
Multiplying,
Subtracting, dividing,
Adding,
Equations,
Modes, medians, means.
You never know, let's go!
Run!
Sigh!
It's party day, hooray!

Heidi Clare Sholl (11)
Chasetown Specialist Sports College, Chasetown

I Can't Write A Poem

Sitting down with a pen in hand, wondering what to write,
Staring at a blank sheet, under my small light.
Shall I write a sonnet, a limerick or a haiku
Or something else? I can't think what to do!

I can't write a poem, I don't know what to do,
Should I write a poem? I might be going cuckoo!

I don't know how they do it, those ever famous bards
Cos when I try to write a poem, I just find it all too hard.
But wait . . .
I'm writing a poem, hooray!
There's something you don't see each day!

I can write a poem, I just didn't see it coming.
I was writing, trying to think of something, then I started humming!

Sean Corbett (12)
Chasetown Specialist Sports College, Chasetown

49

Talk

You can talk all day
You can talk all night
You can talk at the park
You can talk on a flight

You can talk on the phone
You can talk at the pub
You can talk at work
You can talk having a hug

I've just seen a BT advert
According to them you can talk all the time
Ha, ha, ha, ha, ha!
You can talk whenever you want
Wherever you want
About whatever you want
Just talk.

Chloe Matthews (12)
Chasetown Specialist Sports College, Chasetown

2010

2010 times have come,
They bring joy and lots of fun.
It comes so fast and goes so quick,
You're another year older in a tick.
New school year once again,
New cocky year 7s, such a pain!
Walking around town saying, 'Happy New Year!'
It's nice to see everybody in the spirit of cheer.
People all happy and being all kind
Around my area very usual to find.
The area I live in isn't the best,
The teenagers round here just don't give it a rest.
At New Year they should be at home
With family and friends and unable to roam.
2010 times have come.

Alex Taylor (12)
Chasetown Specialist Sports College, Chasetown

Poppi My Puppy

Poppi is my puppy, I love her so, so much!
She sleeps at the bottom of my bed and chews her foot!
She is the runt of the litter but can be a little critter!

I love my puppy Poppi, she barks and also chews all her toys.
When we take her for a walk with the other male dogs she loves it
with the boys.
She is so, so cute and a bundle of fluff
But when she sees my other dogs going out she runs round the
house going *ruff, ruff!*

I love my puppy Poppi, she is so cute
She is very clever but cannot play the flute.
She always follows me round the house but in the back garden she
plays hide in little hollows.
I really love my puppy Poppi, I love her so, so much
She sleeps at the bottom of my bed and always chews her foot!

Natalie Evans (12)
Chasetown Specialist Sports College, Chasetown

Winter

We must put our summer things away
It's time to put on our hats and scarves
Winter is here, hip, hip, hooray!

'Look Mom, there's no school today
Can we build a snowman?'
'Just wrap up warm you can go and play.'

Does your snowman have a woolly hat?
Does your snowman have a button mouth?
Does your snowman have a snow cat?

What about a snowball fight?
That sounds fun
Hide, duck, run!
Make lots of snowballs round and white.

Luke Yeomans-Smith (12)
Chasetown Specialist Sports College, Chasetown

51

My Parcel

I once was expecting a parcel
From a company called Marcel.
It arrived quite late
I was extremely irate
It turned out to be Microsoft Excel.

I decided to make a complaint
But I was feeling extremely faint.
I fell to the floor
Unable to get to the door
And declared computers no saint.

My parcel turned out to be
A rip-off I now see
So I threw it out
Of my cousin's house
And now my computer is dead, tee, he, he!

Emily Bone (12)
Chasetown Specialist Sports College, Chasetown

Our World

As I look at the sky I feel the temptation
Then I look at them and I see the imitation
I look around at the world I see
Nothing but hatred and cruelty.

People laugh, people cry,
People live, people die.

The rivers flow and the sun beams
But as the sun shines, our world screams.
The black inky clouds cover the sea
Which makes the future shorter for you and me.

Our world laughs, our world cries,
Our world lives and it dies,
Our world.

Grace Newbury (13)
Chasetown Specialist Sports College, Chasetown

Maddie

Oh Maddie, oh Maddie, where did you go?
You disappeared down the garden to play with the snow.
When I found you, you were behind the shed,
Growling at next-door's cat named Fred.
I tried to grab you but you ran away
Found a stick and started to play.
You ran round in circles dodging past me
The back door opened and out came my brother Lee.
He picked up your ball to play some more
But unfortunately it was time for tea.
Sausage, chips and a big pork chop
You sat and waited for a bit to drop.
You dribbled and drooled but we weren't fooled
You were getting nothing but your tinned dog food!

Shannon Evans (12)
Chasetown Specialist Sports College, Chasetown

The Perfect Pair

I am so tall, I am so high,
You can see me passing by.
In my favourite pair of heels
Down the High Street I go.

In my wedges, in my heels,
Round and round go the wheels.
In the limo, out I come,
In my perfect high-heeled shoes.

I am so loud, I am so proud,
I think that I impressed the crowd.
If they're stilettos, boots or wedges
I will always love my shoes.

Ellie Jupp (12)
Chasetown Specialist Sports College, Chasetown

The Famous Aston Villa

In 1874, the club was founded
Football was set alive
All teams shook with lots of fear
The fans help this club survive.

In 1982 we played Munich
European Cup final day.
We won the match by one goal to nil
Come on you Villa boys . . . yeah!

Now we are here in 2010
Agbonlahor, Milner and Dunne
They pick up the ball, they shoot, they score!
And Aston Villa have won!

Ben Green (14)
Chasetown Specialist Sports College, Chasetown

The Girl Across The Street

The girl from across the street slept with a ruler to see how long she slept!
When she took me to the airport saw a sign that said, 'Airport left'
And turned round to go home!
The girl from across the street studied for a blood test!
She stared at her orange juice because it said concentrate!
She called me to ask my new number, the girl from across the street!
She tried to drown a fish and put M&Ms in alphabetical order!
She missed the 44 bus so she took the 22 bus twice!
The girl from across the street starved to death locked in a supermarket!
The girl from across the street was the stupidest girl I know!

Cloe Astbury (12)
Chasetown Specialist Sports College, Chasetown

Cats!

Sleeping softly on the bed,
His whiskers twitching harmlessly,
His beautiful fur shimmering
In the golden rays of light.
I stroke his curled back
And he stretches and yawns.
He stands up and then lies on my lap,
He closes his eyes and falls asleep.
His tummy going up and down,
Pressing against mine.
I love my cat, my purrfect cat,
My black and white three-legged cat.

Olivia Seager (11)
Chasetown Specialist Sports College, Chasetown

Life

The meaning behind it
Is to enjoy
To find friendship
To have good laughs
Be responsible
To have hope
You're only here once!

Rhys Chatterfield (14)
Chasetown Specialist Sports College, Chasetown

Art!

I love to doodle, I love to draw
And I used to paint on the bathroom door.
But now I am older I have had to learn
That maybe back then I took the wrong turn.
So now I like to be precise
And always get my work just right.

Mollie Johnson (12)
Chasetown Specialist Sports College, Chasetown

55

A Young Boy

There was a young boy of nine
Whose limerick was perfectly fine.
He started to write
On a dark winter's night
But couldn't think of a last line!

Alex Carroll (14)
Chasetown Specialist Sports College, Chasetown

A Summer Full Of Love

The sun was shining as bright as the beautiful sky
As the breeze came through the day
The birds were singing
The clock was ringing
The lovely day went away.

Next day you could see trees
Swaying, swaying away
There was the valley
In front of the galley
I wanted the sun to stay.

Night sky came and arrived
As the sun went down to sleep
There was no talking
Or a bird squawking
Your heart is the thing you can keep.

Chanelle Amber Harley (11)
Chesterton Community Sports College, Chesterton

The Sea

The calm blue sea sloshing in the breeze
Peacefully the small waves rolled over the sand
Then quietly the small waves slowly rolled back out to sea.

In the clear air I could smell the salt drifting from the ocean
In the distance I saw the bright sun beaming down onto the glistening sea
It looked like diamonds sparkling on a winter day in the snow.

As I looked around there was just me standing there on the soft, crumbling sand
And the small waves rolling on my feet.
In the distance there were white seagulls diving into the sea to catch the small blue fish.

Suddenly the sea turned rough and the waves crashed,
Bashed against the jagged rocks on the coast.
They were fierce like a roaring lion in the jungle,
The tide came in quickly, loudly, the waves were everywhere.

A big wave hit the rock, I could taste the salt as it splashed in my mouth, it was horrible.
I touched the wet soft sand, it felt slimy, there was seaweed all over the place.
I touched it, it was slimy, smelly and really disgusting.
The waves calmed down and I walked off slowly into the distance of the beach.

James Brayford (12)
Chesterton Community Sports College, Chesterton

9/11 Disaster!

Nine eleven was a disaster
The planes and Towers met.
The passengers weren't aware
As they worked and sat.

The passengers were ready
To go to somewhere hot
To enjoy themselves and have fun
But controllers of planes lost the plot.

New York was a busy place
Nowhere to mess about
But they knew what they were doing
And started to set out.

As the workers worked
They thought it was a normal day
But they never would have thought
This was the price to pay.

The Towers got so close
The workers and passengers cry.
The victims picked up the phone
To say their goodbyes.

One of the planes got stopped
But unfortunately crashed.
All of the passengers died
This day lasts and lasts.

The Towers crumbled and cracked
Suddenly fell to the floor.
There was not much time
To escape out of the door.

So that was the day of the 9/11 disaster
Their families were sad
They loved them so much.
But hopefully now it's not as bad.

Alice Rhodes (12)
Chesterton Community Sports College, Chesterton

The Rose

I am a rose, big, bold and brass
Sitting outside a shop feeling all alone
Then one day somebody came and picked me up
Take me home, I thought, *take me home.*

Once I was home in the warmth I went to bed
Sitting in a vase with water waiting to be fed
Then I heard a voice shouting, 'Wait, wait!'

She got me out of the vase and took me back with her
Down by the riverside she went
Out in the cold with frost on my nose
She jumped in and swam away never to be seen again

Then I thought, *how could she leave?*
My petals are as red as new crafted rubies
I'm as slender as a slither of frost on my nose
Delicate as a newborn babe
My thorns are as sharp as pin's head
And after all I'm as elegant as a ballerina

As I lay there in the cold, the frost began to trickle off my nose
Like a tear running down somebody's face
My petals began to drop off like somebody dropping stones
Then I began to die, the cold hitting me like nothing I have ever felt
before
I thought, *I have never had a life*
As the night began to fall I was getting weaker and weaker
This is the end, I thought and then suddenly . . . I stopped breathing.

Kyra Oakes (12)
Chesterton Community Sports College, Chesterton

King Kong

As the tide blew in, the boat was ready to go
A big roar and the tide was low
A swaying flow and a boat could move
A wild ocean and rocks up against the flow.

As the boat turned into the cave
All the crew got off to discover
As they passed the native gate
A lava temple like no other.

A giant rattle in the forest
And soon a ferocious roar
A black shadow in the distance
The tribesmen scattered to houses and more.

A dancing woman on the cliff edge
A great big gorilla made a crack
As she jumped and fell
A great leap, the monster went back.

A T-rex was a challenge
But the gorilla could manage
A couple of scratches, nothing too much
A good result for a dinosaur so savage.

An unsafe log going to a cave
TheN a roar and a great push
They feLl down into a bog
And they knew they must rush.

Surrounded by unknown creatures
Big and small
All surrounding them
They were scared of them all.

They got out of the horrible swamp
As they got to the boat
A man turned round and went to look
Hoping that she wasn't in a lava moat.

He finally reached the tip of Skull Island
A big gorilla lying on the floor
As he crept up to the beast
The eyes of the gorilla opened some more.

The monster was mad
Jumping around
They tranquilised him
Down to the ground . . .

Dominic Lucas (11)
Chesterton Community Sports College, Chesterton

War Has Come

Clink . . .
As the train started to move
Tears ran down his face
Each drip smelling of fire
As he arrived in his new town
He found war was breaking loose
As bombs hit the beach
Forcing him to his home
His new parents shouting, 'Poor Tommy.'
Tommy headed for war at the age of twelve
Killing all the people in his way
He ran to stop the Germans in World War II
If only he had stopped, he wouldn't be dead!

Kieren Williams (11)
Chesterton Community Sports College, Chesterton

Stoke City FC V Arsenal FC

Stoke City kick off
Pass it around
And they break and it goes out
And there's a Rory Delap throw inbound

Rory Delap throws it in
Fuller just heads it in
And it's in the back of the net
Arsenal are throwing everything in the bin

And now it's a bad tackle by Danny Collins
And it's a free kick
Passed to Denilson and shoots
And it's a goal from a deflected flick

And now it's half time
And the Stoke fans are loving it
Arsenal might lose
At the moment Arsenal are stuck in a pit

The players are coming out
And it kicks off
With Arsenal once again
The Arsenal fans start to scoff

It starts well
Both teams have had lots of possession
Mainly Stoke
And there's going to be a lot of aggression

Fuller's getting a lot of chances
But just not scoring
Fuller's hoping for a hat-trick
So far it's been boring

Fuller scores again
The Stoke fans are amazed
It's Mamady Sidibe that gets the assist
The volume has been raised

Again a goal from Stoke
Dean Whitehead this time
The fans are going mad
As their glory starts to climb

The final whistle goes
And now it's time to go for the Arsenal fans
Time to go
Stoke will be making plans!

Jack Stokes (11)
Chesterton Community Sports College, Chesterton

Bradwell Bombers

B radwell Bombers
R aging through the roaring crowd
A t half time we have a drink
D oing what we've been told
W inning for the crowd
E ach of us training hard
L earning how to do things better
L aughing and having a joke

B anging the goals in
O h we are a good team!
M eaning what we do
B ringing in new players
E ncouraging ourselves
R unning through our operations
S o we are the Bradwell Bombers and we are proud!

Ben Kinnersley (12)
Chesterton Community Sports College, Chesterton

Titanic

The Titanic
Was built in Belfast
The passengers loved it
It was all in the past.

They thought it was unsinkable
They were wrong.
On that day
They were waiting very long.

2,223 were on board
They didn't know that their lives were on the line.
On that dreadful day
All the children were mostly nine.

The Titanic
Was built in Belfast
The passengers loved it
It was all in the past.

On 14th April, 1912
They were shouting names
On that dreadful day
Then the iceberg came.

The lives were lost of 1,517
The lifeboats were not full
Women and children went first
They pulled and pulled.

The Titanic
Was built in Belfast
The passengers loved it
It was all in the past.

The iceberg came so fast
The Titanic is history
They didn't know what was going on
It was a mystery.

The Titanic had a sister
That sunk as well
2 hours and 40 minutes it took
It was hard to tell.

The Titanic
Was built in Belfast
The passengers loved it
It was all in the past.

Kimberly Mason (11)
Chesterton Community Sports College, Chesterton

The Sea

The dark blue sea is bright and beautiful
The peaceful way the waves move
It tastes horrible and tastes like salt
You feel the slimy touch of the crabs and the slimy touch of the rocks
The waves clash together like somebody hitting a drum
The sand is soft, when the sun hits the sand
It becomes warm like a cup of tea in the morning
The pebbles are hard and rough like the sea
And that is the sea and the way it moves.

Molly Tyas (11)
Chesterton Community Sports College, Chesterton

Snow White

Snow White was a fair young maiden,
Whose father sadly passed away.
So her evil stepmother took over
Trying to control her in every way.

But the queen was jealous of her beauty,
She wanted the young maiden dead
So she sent the woodcutter out to return with her heart,
But he brought back a pig's heart instead.

Snow White fled far from the palace
For she was scared of the queen's jealousy.
Only to find a small cottage
Where she thought she was destined to be.

Snow White thought she was in this house alone
But there was a huge surprise in store.
For she heard a lot of voices
As seven little men walked through the door.

She was happy when they let her stay
She thought she owed them a favour
So she called on her animal friends
To help give the house a tasteful flavour.

Back at the palace the queen's anger started to show
When she looked in the mirror
And she saw Snow White
In the cottage cleaning with a baby deer.

So the queen put on a cunning disguise
And began to carry out her plan
Of poisoning the princess
Thinking that she can.

She went to the young girl's cottage
With a poisoned apple In her hand
And watched and waited with pleasure
As the young girl fell into the land.

But just as she was placed into a glass case
There came a prince on a trusty steed
Who leant down and kissed her
So the happily ever after was achieved.

Jasmine Wootton (12)
Chesterton Community Sports College, Chesterton

Alphabetical Poem

A is for a tiny ant
B is for a buzzing bee
C is for a very fat cat
D is for a kind dad
E is for a very tiny elephant
F is for fast food
G is for grazing goat
H is for an amazing holly tree
I is for a beautiful island
J is for a big jam jar
K is for a dome kid
L is for a tasty lollipop
M is for a massive mug
N is for a chicken nugget
O is for a massive orange
P is for a pretty red poppy
Q is for our smashing Queen
R is for a fast roller coaster
S is for a slimy snake
T is for a peeping Tom
U is for a beautiful umbrella
V is for our Queen Victoria
W is for a wicked witch
X is for a big x-ray
Y is for a fantastic yo-yo
Z is for a fast zebra.

Tom Green (12)
Chesterton Community Sports College, Chesterton

Animals

A is the amazing armadillo
B is for the bombing bat
C is for the cute cuddly cat
D is for the dancing dodo
E is for the enormous elephant
F is for the fantastic fish
G is for gaggling goose
H is for the happy horse
I is for the incredible impala
J is for the jumping jaguar
K is for the kicking kangaroo
L is for the leaping lion
M is for the mini mouse
N is for the nice newt
O is for the octuple octopus
P is for the pouncing penguin
Q is for the queen bee
R is for the running rabbit
S is for the swimming swan
T is for the tapping toad
U is for unau
V is for vixen
W is for whale
X is for X-ray fish
Y is for yak
Z is for zebra.

Sian Simm (11)
Chesterton Community Sports College, Chesterton

The News

I turn on the TV
Watch the news for a change
The names that they say
Seem so different and strange.

There are so many faces
They all look so sad
It's like the world
Is just going mad.

There are fires and floods
The earthquake is new
So many have died
Are you glad it's not you?

Tornadoes and famine
Take a grip of the Earth
People are running
For all that they're worth.

With all the disasters
The world seems so sad
Still fighting a war
Are they really that mad?

So when you sit down
And watch the programmes you choose
Just think of the people
That are making the news.

Scott Paterson (12)
Chesterton Community Sports College, Chesterton

The Waggerdodo
(Based on 'Jabberwocky' by Lewis Carroll)

'Twas a bogiley night
Did wogiley and dogiley in the wackojogey
All jangerly came the waggerdogo
And the people ran shouting
Clunk, clunk, bonk, bonk.

Beware of the waggerdogo, my daughter
The jaws that catch, the claws that kill,
Beware of the tubtub bird.

By the night-time she went
Crash, bang, wallop, dead!

Hooray, good day my bashous girl
Who killed the waggerdogo
My daughter.

Rebecca Pagett (11)
Chesterton Community Sports College, Chesterton

Samuel

S uper Sam down the wing
A ttacking the ball
M aking trys all day long
U sing my loud voice
E ven hurting myself
L ooking around.

Samuel Blundall (11)
Chesterton Community Sports College, Chesterton

70

World War Disaster

1939, Churchill declared war
The Germans took most of Europe
But the Germans wanted more.

Hitler, the Austrian politician
He invaded countries on the beach, on the sand.
Big countries he invaded,
Such as Netherlands, Denmark and Poland.

He joined the Nazis around 1919
The meanest, evilest man the world had ever seen
And he wanted glory, more and more for the German team.

The World War started in 1939
At the Battle of the Atlantic, it was just manic.
The Nazis took on the Canadian, British and US
For the Nazis this was a big, big test.

On the first of September, 1939
Britain evacuated the children
And the women became workmen
Hitler told himself, 'Britain is mine.'

On the tenth of May, 1940
Churchill became Prime Minister
On the 26th the Battle of Dunkirk
Hitler must have had on his face a smirk.

On the 6th of June, 1944
British soldiers landed in France
To get the Nazis off the land
And give the French it back.

D-Day went on for a total of a day
But people in Britain thought it was longer than that
But the soldiers cleared the Nazis off.

Hitler took pills
And committed suicide
Britain had victory over the Germans
And the parties went on outside.

Thomas Cooper (12)
Chesterton Community Sports College, Chesterton

Cool Runnings

Cool Runnings is all about
A Jamaican team
Trying to get in an Olympic race
And they are all very keen

A young man is scared of his dad
For all his life is mixed up
Then one day his dad finds out
That really he is in a bobsleigh cup

When they find their coach to be
Their hope is to be a bobsleigh team
When they start to practise
They are all began to beam

When they start to race
They end up being the best
But then one race
They're up for a test

But when they start to race
They end up being bait
When they let the Jamaicans down
They are still all mates

But then they try for the second time
And they never look back
For all their lives
They have only been treated like tack

Then the crowd goes wild
To know that Cool Runnings are on next
When they have got halfway through
The bobsleigh tips up

The crowd boo
When they see the bobsleigh tip up
It isn't their fault
And they know they'll never give up!

Lara King (11)
Chesterton Community Sports College, Chesterton

Tsunami

It was in Indonesia
No one knew it was going to come on Boxing Day
It was in 2004
But when it came they didn't know what to say.

It was an earthquake that made it occur
It was all a disaster
People didn't know what it was
When it came it came faster and faster.

All it was to them was a shock
Then they noticed that it was 21 feet
People went to go and hide
All they heard was their heartbeat.

Not many people lived
Only 160,000 were spared
It killed 280,000 people,
Family and friends cared.

It was in Indonesia
No one knew it was going to come on Boxing Day
It was in 2004
But when it came they didn't know what to say.

The children were so scared
They didn't know what to do
They had to cling on
All the adults were scared too.

All the children were afraid
Most of them were lost
Their lives will not be the same
Not at any cost.

It was in Indonesia
All those tears and cries
All those people who tried to hold on
Didn't get to say goodbye.

Tania Kwiatkowski (12)
Chesterton Community Sports College, Chesterton

Titanic Ballad

Once the Titanic was constructed it left Liverpool to Berlin
And set sail to Berlin
There it set sail to New York
The sea was peaceful and Titanic was in for the win.

The Atlantic was cold and calm, lovely salty air
In that sea there was a terror waiting
In the depths of the sea
The captain was hating.

Hating the horrible darkness in the deep blue sea
The ball in the ship's mess deck at full blast
Then suddenly bang
Then the ship sank fast.

The ship screamed and the hull was destroyed
The ship wrecked and snapped
The bystanders screamed
The captain did nothing but tap.

Tap the dash on the ship's computers
The violinists played
The people screamed
For it was their last day.

The innocent scrambled
Scrambled into the boat
The men got left behind
Finally they set off and floated.

The women and children settled
The men scattered
Scattered to the five boats left
Then the cold rain pattered.

After two hours the Titanic was dead
Now at the depths of the sea
Now rescued the people are better
Years later it would be the size of a pea.

Jacob Michael Shutt (11)
Chesterton Community Sports College, Chesterton

9/11, The Story No One Will Forget

September 11th, a tragic story
Which no one will forget.
They made many films of this tragedy
Excellent was the set.

Three buildings were involved
Both World Trade Center buildings and the Pentagon were hit
Everyone was shocked and people were in bits.

A lot of people died, you'll never guess how many
3000 people died.
You wouldn't think that much
Everyone around there just sat and cried.

A terrorist group was responsible
Al-Qaeda is their name.
Now because of this there is a war
Life in Afghanistan will never be the same.

But on one plane that was 'jacked'
Brave passengers took back the plane.
Many children, without parents,
Their lives again will never be the same.

Because of this tragic event
People were waiting for a call.
People sat on the edge of their seat
But unfortunately, sadness for all.

Memories were held around the world
To bless the wonderful lives
Of all people on September 11th
Who lost their life.

So this concludes my story
At this tragic time
Always remember the souls
Who were out of time.

Owain Shenton (11)
Chesterton Community Sports College, Chesterton

Twilight Ballad

Bella moves to Forks
And falls in love
And thinks that it is
A message from above

Bella has no idea
That her future love has
A secret, she thinks
He is normal and not at all bad

His charms are strong
And his looks are stunning
But while she falls in love
She has to keep on running

Bella has a taste for danger
Getting involved with a vampire
Her life gets stranger
As he keeps going higher

The trackers are after her
Her life in danger
Edward tries to keep her safe
But only for a time remainder

Edward and the Cullens
Fight to help Bella
And keep her safe
And with her fella

One of the trackers has been destroyed
With nothing left of him but ash
They ripped him apart and burnt the remains
And now he's just a bit of trash.

Natalie Wright (12)
Chesterton Community Sports College, Chesterton

Animal Alphabet

A is for ant, a small insect that lives on the floor
B is for a bully bee who stings
C is for a cute cat
D is for a lovely dog
E is for evil elephant
F is for frog
G is for a gorilla
H is for a beautiful hamster
 I is for an insect
J is for a jaguar
K is for a bouncy kangaroo
L is for a slippery lizard
M is for a swinging monkey
N is for a smooth newt
O is for a slimy octopus
P is for a talking parrot
Q is for a scary queen snake
R is for a rodent rat
S is for a creepy spider
T is for a predator tiger
U is for a fairy tale unicorn
V is for a bloodsucking vampire bat
W is for a man-eating werewolf
X is for a transparent X-ray fish
Y is for a hidden dragon called Yinlong
Z is for a stripy zebra.

Michael Tennant (11)
Chesterton Community Sports College, Chesterton

Haiku Poem

The rain is heavy
The clouds covering the sun
The sun is coming.

Anthony Sims (11)
Chesterton Community Sports College, Chesterton

My Hero

3, 2, 1, go, the smell of burning rubber
The race has begun, here they come
Into the first corner,
Hope there's nothing bad
As they come round there is little drama
They all make it round the first corner
But that's only the first part
As they pass through the chicane
There is a spin
Then a bang
When I look there are two cars
They have crashed
The recovery goes to clear the track
Before you know it they have cleared the track
Before the cars come back round
Over the radio there is a thank you
They tow the car round to paddock
And then return to their place
So I run to the truck and it is my grandad's truck
I think in my head, he's a hero
And I will never forget that day out
To Oulton Park race circuit.

Connor Montford (13)
Chesterton Community Sports College, Chesterton

Everlasting Love

F orever and ever
A lways there to help you when you're in trouble
M any hugs and kisses
I love my family with all my heart
L ots of Sunday dinners
Y ou always know you can count on them

F un and exciting
R eliable
I love my friends
E ntertaining when you're sad
N ever let you down
D on't ever take them for granted
S ometimes you argue but you always make up

P recious - when you're sad they comfort you
E nergetic and playful is my dog Holly
T G is my hamster's name
S oft and fluffy and full of fun

So what I am trying to say here is that you shouldn't push them away,
They're the ones you should keep close each and every day.

Emily Fay Parry (11)
Chesterton Community Sports College, Chesterton

Wonderful Things

Friends are there for you,
Friends never let you down.
Friends cheer you up when you are feeling blue,
My friends I can trust all of the time.
My friends are hilarious, they make me laugh,
My friends are caring and kind.

Pets are very funny and can be hyperactive,
Pets are soft, fluffy and cuddly.
Pets cheer you up and give you a big sloppy kiss.
Pets are friendly; my dog defends my family by guarding us.
My pets, I truly love, I couldn't ask for better pets,
My pets I know they will always be there for me!

Family cares for you.
Family love and look after you and make sure you are OK.
Family are always there for you no matter what.
My family are kind, truthful and help me too.
My family support me and stand up for me.
My family are the best
So I'd just like to say thank you for these wonderful, fantastic, brilliant things!

Leigh Williams (11)
Chesterton Community Sports College, Chesterton

The Glorious Cat

The cat's eyes sparkled like diamonds; he looked very fluffy, fluffier than a teddy to a pillow
He smelt like coconut shampoo from when he had a bath.
I could also smell cat food from when he had his dinner and his fur was soft, softer than silk
I could hear the glorious cat purring,
It sounded like someone playing a cello and it hissed, it sounded like he was talking to me.
The glorious cat would not harm you, he would help you.
That is one glorious cat.

Sam Wales (11)
Chesterton Community Sports College, Chesterton

Football, Football, What A Game

Football, football, what a game
I love it so much, it keeps me sane
The beautiful game
Is the best
No one is better than Georgie Best.

The pitch is vast
Forget the past
England will score with a blast
They are so very fast
And save the day.

Rooney, Rooney all the way
Goes for the shot and saves the day!
A striking force ten today
Eleven with a sub, hip, hip hooray!

The crowd cheering all the way
As their season tickets blow away
Red faces because it is cold today
England will win, hip, hip hooray!

Joel Sanderson (11)
Chesterton Community Sports College, Chesterton

Love Poem

There is a nice girl over there
But I don't want to stare
I like her a lot because she is hot
I don't know if she likes me
But I like her
I hope it is the same way for me
When the day comes
I'll go up to her
With lots of glee
I hope the day comes
And I hope she loves me.

Lloyd Dawson (12)
Chesterton Community Sports College, Chesterton

Spider-Man

Along came a spider that bit his limb
It only dropped from behind him.
Little did he know a robber was on foot
All he could do was tut.
There he saw Uncle Ben on the floor
All he did was let the robber out the door.
The lake of blood was like a big great flood.
His thoughts were a-blobber
He knew it was the robber.
As Spider-Man grew and grew
He was becoming new all through.
In love with Mary-Jane,
Life will never be the same.
As he makes the suit
His voice is on mute.
The robber is dead
With blood on his head.
The mystery is still on
Is it a con?

Thomas Bennett (11)
Chesterton Community Sports College, Chesterton

I Love Animals

Roar goes the hungry lion
Purr goes the happy cat
Hiss goes the slithery snake
Moo goes the nagging cow
Grunt goes the greedy pig
Buzz goes the buzzing bee
Croak goes the crazy frog
Growl goes the loud dog
Neigh goes the grumpy horse
Tu-whit tu-whoo goes the noisy owl.
I love animals!

Courtney Simcock (11)
Chesterton Community Sports College, Chesterton

World War I

Smoke through the battlefield
As gunners try to shoot you down
But the enemy will not yield
You see enemy planes bombing your town

Gas killing innocent men, women and children
People can't breathe in the toxic fumes
Men trying to put their masks on
But they have already breathed in the fumes

Men hiding in a trench
Shooting for their lives
They wish they were sat on a peaceful bench
Men can no longer dive

Women and children crying
Whilst the dad is dying
Left on their own
They will never give up on their husbands.

Dominic Pepe (12)
Chesterton Community Sports College, Chesterton

How Do You Know?

How do you know when you will witness something amazing or
devastating?
How do you know when you hear something terrifying or something
beautiful?
How do you know if God is real or not?
How do you know who is right and who is wrong?
How do you know when someone will get injured or get saved?
How do you know when you will die?
That's the thing with these things, you don't!

William Scott Lloyd Stanier (11)
Chesterton Community Sports College, Chesterton

I Love Animals

The chirp of a bird
The roar of a lion
The hiss of a snake
The snort of a pig
The howl of a fox
The laugh of a monkey
The buzz of a wasp
The squeak of a mouse
The twitter of an owl
The bark of a dog
The snap of a crocodile's jaw
The baa of a sheep
The croak of a frog
The moo of a cow
The whistle of a blackbird
The purr of a cat.
I love animals!

Hadleigh Brentnall (12)
Chesterton Community Sports College, Chesterton

The Silence Of The Moon At Night

Owls tweet as a wolf pack eats
In the silence of the moon at night.
Coal leaps as the fire gives off heat while moths scatter as
spiderwebs shatter
In the silence of the moon at night.
Dogs bark as the day turns dark
In the silence of the moon at night.
Dragonflies make quick fire dashes as elephants stomp and make
hundreds of splashes
In the silence of the moon at night.
As the moon disappears behind the clouds, the forest is illuminated
with the energy
In the silence of the moon at night.

Jake Lovatt (11)
Chesterton Community Sports College, Chesterton

Alpha Poem

A is for apples which are either red or green
B is for bananas which make scared people scream like mad - *argh!*
C is for cherries that taste so good - *wow!*
D is for danger - it always strikes in the woods!
E is for endings with everything brought on the way
F is for friendships that light up the day
G is for gold which is such an incredible thing
H is for hours, the days go so quickly they make you go ding!
I is for insects which look quite strong - not!
J is for joggers, you'd better get the routine right you lot!
K is for kings which rule our precious land
L is for luxury - never do it by hand
M is for mountains that rise above you
N is for near the mountains are collapsing in two
O is for orange, I'm not speaking French!
P is for power, you could be so lucky for the special things
    you receive!

Rebecca Green (11)
Chesterton Community Sports College, Chesterton

The Sand

It is a yellow orange colour; it looks as soft as velvet!
Just looking at it you can see the steam rising from it, it is boiling!
As I slowly step onto it I can hear the crunching
Of the tiny bits of gravel cracking in-between my toes.
When I bend down to pick some of it up,
It feels really smooth, just like silk, my hands are red raw,
I have to drop it, it is too hot!
Quickly I run and jump into the sea; my feet are blistered and sore.
In the sea all I can taste is salt, it is disgusting!
My feet are all moulded into it; it was all soft and wet.
Every time I take a step it tickled my feet
It is the sand!

Tia Stephanie Walker (12)
Chesterton Community Sports College, Chesterton

Earthquake In Haiti

There was a rumble, then a crumble
I was lying in bed next to my teddy called Ted
I could feel the ground shaking
Then I knew that something bad was quaking
I could see buildings crumbling
Then they started tumbling
Suddenly people started running
And soon were fumbling
I could taste the pure dust in the air
Then I thought, this isn't fair
A slight smell of rubble and dust
On the metal I could see a lot of rust
After the quake
I started to shake
There were loads of fatal accidents.

David Jones (12)
Chesterton Community Sports College, Chesterton

I Like Noise

The start of the day a bang!
I heard a car near to the school crash.
I was in my classroom, my teacher shouting at us
Then I heard the bang again.
Then I heard two new noises, boom and pop!
The sound I heard, it was a car or a kid making a bang, boom and pop!
I like noise.

Liam Faram (12)
Chesterton Community Sports College, Chesterton

Noise Poem

I like noise . . .

The switching on of the lights
Shimmering like stars
The hubbub of children
The beeping of cars
Doors slamming
Feet clattering
People shouting on their way to class
Papers rustling
Pages turning
Equipment rattling in the box
Keyboards tapping, projectors humming
High heels tapping on the tiles.

I like noise.

Courtney Harris (12)
Chesterton Community Sports College, Chesterton

Noise Poem

I like noise
The children are rushing and raving to class
There goes the bell, Year 7s giggling to their class
Lining up outside the class when some let out an evil laugh
Thud, thud, thud, up and up
Bang, bang, bang as the door collapses
Keyboards tapping, mouse wiggling one more time they will be
collapsing.

Cars beeping and cats screaming
Pitter-patters on the roof
The teachers telling them to ignore the roof
When it is 3pm the children say, 'Hooray, hooray, it is the end of the
day'
So they can go out and play.

Bethany Dale (12)
Chesterton Community Sports College, Chesterton

8 Aynsley

There's a class in CCSC who
Have a fab English teacher

In her class she has 23 kids
Oh, what a sight! Some talk,
Some chew and sometimes don't listen,
But most of them are well-behaved.

In her class she has a group of girls who flirt with all the boys
And a group of boys who always play on games.
But in this class she has a big group of kids
Who do what she says.

At the end of the day she will always say,
'Oh 8 Aynsley, what a day we have had
I am hoping to see you tomorrow.'

Marie Parry (13)
Chesterton Community Sports College, Chesterton

My Friend

My friend has gone to a happier place
She went to Heaven above
I will never be able to replace
She was a nice old love
I can't even picture her face
She has gone for good
For the better and worst
I will never forget her
She was driven off in a hearse
She was laid to rest in her nice comfy dress
My friend.

Amber Nelson (12)
Chesterton Community Sports College, Chesterton

The Zibomagbos
(Based on 'Jabberwocky' by Lewis Carroll)

On the chips and trimbee day
The zibomagbos came to Jimo's fimotams
Where all the abogobbles were boogling tibleticks
It was severabo and the bobletick was setting
It was pimtickles in the bibblebab.

'Beware of the simbo-tangon
As it will gobble you like a timbo-wang!
Take limboodeas as the day passes
Or else you will be ashes.'

As though he said, 'You will be dead'
He was the one who disboggled
He ended up dead with a slah on his head
And was found chimboed in the picco-east way.

Chelsea Brandall (11)
Chesterton Community Sports College, Chesterton

Best Friends

He sat in the corner just staring at me,
His eyes bright and shiny as red as can be.
He had long scaly fingers and green bumpy skin,
It gave me the shivers just looking at him.
I looked at him closely and quietly said,
'What have you just said?'
I stepped back once, I stepped back twice
As I did he shouted, 'Boo!'
I ran round the room like a scared mouse,
It was like he was in the whole house!

Charlotte Smith (13)
Chesterton Community Sports College, Chesterton

Waterfalls

W onderful water splashing
A lways crashing and smells fresh
T earing everything in half
E very part is lovely
R efreshing water
F alling everywhere
A lways flowing
L ovely smell
L ike the sea.

Connah Lucas (11)
Chesterton Community Sports College, Chesterton

Bullies

Bullies, bullies, they're very bad
Bullies, bullies, they leave you feeling sad.
The bullies, bullies are coming for you
Quick, hide, before they find you.

But then someone comes along
And turns that frown upside down.
They have left me feeling fearless and strong.

Leanne Banks (12)
Chesterton Community Sports College, Chesterton

Pixie Place

You see the bright lights of their wings
Glistening in the wind like freshly cleaned diamonds
Wings as soft as velvet as you stroke across them
The bright red cherry lips
The scent of the flowers as they gently fly by you with their delicate
bodies
They glance at you with their beautiful rosy red faces.

Hannah Warner (12)
Chesterton Community Sports College, Chesterton

The Snow

It started snowing very heavily at night
So when I woke up the sight was snow
It was quite deep
They shone like crystals in the ground
So I grabbed my sledge and I sat on my behind
I pushed so hard to go down and down the hill
Swirling around and around like a tornado and *bang!* I was done.

Jessica Gibson (13)
Chesterton Community Sports College, Chesterton

The Beach

The sun was blazing hot
Looking down on the children in the sea
As I sat under the palm tree
I watched them carefully

The glistening sand felt hot on my feet
Playing games, oh it was so great!

Storm Jeana Sargeant (12)
Chesterton Community Sports College, Chesterton

I Like Noise

Bang goes the ball hitting the net
Thump goes the football player's feet hitting the solid ground
Cheer goes the crowd when the team scores
Splat goes the rain hitting the field
Scream goes the crowd when everyone has to go.
I like noise.

Jack Crewe (12)
Chesterton Community Sports College, Chesterton

91

The Weather

The smell of the fresh winter air
The sound of the rain hitting my window
The sight of me and my friends making a snowman
The taste of ice cream on a summer's day
The touch of the blue sea on holiday
The weather is wonderful!

Caitlin Barry (11)
Chesterton Community Sports College, Chesterton

Bully Poem

B ossy and horrible to others
U mbrella and coat stealing when there's rain
L ucky or unlucky, take your pick
L onely and upset is how the victim feels
Y ou should stick up for yourself.

Leah Bayley (12)
Chesterton Community Sports College, Chesterton

Haiku Poem

The snow whooshed away
The snow whooshed up in the sky
All the snow has gone.

Courtney Evans (11)
Chesterton Community Sports College, Chesterton

Death

Death is inevitable
It happens, a cycle
The cycle of life and death
Some fear it
They hate the fact
That it will happen
That one day, they will go
From here, from everything
Everything they know
Others don't fear it
But accept the dire truth
That they must die
They know it will happen
And that nothing
That nothing can stop it
Some already want it
A chance to end it all
Their life, their existence
Shattered, gone, unwanted
Because of how their life is
How they live
How they are treated
Made to feel that no one cares
That they are unwanted
That there is no purpose
No purpose for them to live
No reason for their life.

Liana Jane Bourne (13)
Clayton Hall Business & Language College, Newcastle

Summer's Day

I woke up on a summer's day
Lying in a cosy warm bed I lay
When the bell suddenly rang
As quick as a flash I sprang
I leapt down the stairs like a frog
Just escaping a collision with my dog.
I finally got to the door
But as I opened it my heart sank to the floor
I was to be a soldier in the war.

Two years on and I'm finally here
My heart dying with fear
Bullets were hitting the ground
Pound after pound after pound
Suddenly someone shouted, 'Gas'
Time started to pass
I tried to put my gas mask on
But my chance had gone
I started gasping for air
Only to fall to the floor in despair.

I awoke on a summer's day
Lying in a cosy warm place I lay
But this time no one was at the door
Apart from every single thing I adore.

James Attwood (13)
Clayton Hall Business & Language College, Newcastle

May

The first day of May is like a new opening of a book
Shepherds begin to get out and use their crook
It's a fresh start and everywhere begins to look smart
The grass turns green and flowers will bud
It's a new life for animals, as it should
Everywhere is colourful and is bright
And the nights begin to be more light.

Molly Ryles (13)
Clayton Hall Business & Language College, Newcastle

The War

We are soldiers going into war,
Lots of bloodshed and hearts are torn.
We leave our lives for our countries thought,
We fight together and stay together.

We lie in filthy foxholes from night to dawn,
With our guns and lives within our thoughts.
We run out shouting, our voices piercing through the air,
Scaring all enemies which lurk there.

I see an enemy coming from behind,
So with my knife it pierces inside.
I see the white of the enemy's eyes
And then I leave him there to die.

He lies dying on the floor,
Soon his heart will beat no more.
I see an enemy dying; no!
Just a man, a father, a son.

What's war worth?
A piece of land, a border moved, a tyrant gone.
The soldier's views are never known,
Follow orders, fight, their dreams of home.

Bradlee Royall (12)
Clayton Hall Business & Language College, Newcastle

Death

Most people do not want to die
And when you do, you cannot cry.
Your body lies there all cold and still,
You are alone; you're all on your bill.
It's black, it's quiet and you are thoughtless
You wish that you had been more cautious.
When you're alive you are really afraid
That the Grim Reaper doesn't take you away.

Sasha Novakovic (13)
Clayton Hall Business & Language College, Newcastle

95

Love Is . . .

Love is long-suffering and is kind,
It is not jealous, it does not mind.
There is no bragging or getting puffed up
That's the way we're supposed to love.
No indecent behaviour, no interests of its own
No being provoked, no being alone.
There's no account of injurious things
It rejoices with truth, happiness it brings
Pursue love 'cause it never gives up
Neither should you when things get tough.
Love is intimate, love never fails
All you need is to balance the scales.
Love is a powerful sate of the heart
Getting it broken can tear you apart.
Love bears all things
Believes all things
Hopes all things
Endures all things.
This is what real love brings.

Elliott Barrow (14)
Clayton Hall Business & Language College, Newcastle

Sacrifice

Sacrifice is a meaningful action
It is always full of mixed emotion.
Pilot, soldier, marine, so much to choose from,
Always to end your life starting from now on.
Making your country proud, they all claimed
However so many died, you're only one out of the million dead.
Consequences worse than before
Families waiting for their dead fathers to come to the door.
'Why must we fight?' the children reply
But it's too late now, the war is on and here to stay for a while.

Léa Sutton (13)
Clayton Hall Business & Language College, Newcastle

Yours Forever

I don't think you will
Ever fully understand
How you've touched my life
And made me who I am.

I don't think you could ever know
Just how truly special you are
Even on my darkest night
You are my brightest star!

You've allowed me to experience
Something hard to find
That love exists
In my body, soul and mind.

I don't think you could ever feel
All the love I have to give
You truly are my will to live
I am forever yours!

Rebecca Swift (13)
Clayton Hall Business & Language College, Newcastle

The Wars Of Our World - Haikus

There is lots of gore
When we fight in a few wars
Deaths fill up the drawers.

When a few sparks fly
The world is going to die
Human deaths are nigh.

Guns and bombs are used
A war cannot be refused
Might have to defuse.

Tanks rumble along
Hoping nothing will go wrong
Soldiers sing a song.

Dominic Moss (12)
Clayton Hall Business & Language College, Newcastle

Summer's Day

Swallows and swifts filled the sky,
Smiled upon by the sun up high.
Flowers filled the garden with colour,
Life could never be any duller.

School was over, fun was here,
As well the sun did appear.
We saw my family almost every day,
This was perfect in every way.

We rode our bikes down by the stream
Whilst fish swam with a shiny gleam.
We climbed trees and ran through the wood
Everything was well and good.

Yet school is again the impurity
Summer is just a memory.
It is just in the past,
Why did summer go so fast?

Mark Bollington (13)
Clayton Hall Business & Language College, Newcastle

Death Not Glory

King and country
Die like poultry
People are dying
Babies crying
Many are dead
It's all in our head
Death is glory
Not that old story
Dead in a ditch
Rot in a ditch
Lying in a pool of blood
Face down in mud
Choose your way to die.

Gabriel Bailey (13)
Clayton Hall Business & Language College, Newcastle

The Truth

They only talk about the victory
Or how good it is to fight for your country
But they never say what it's really like
They never mention the fear that flows through you
When you're standing there like a target
They never say about the regret you have
When you have to leave men behind
They don't know how it feels
When you see your best mate dead on the floor
They don't know what it's like
Knowing that you might not see your family again
They don't know the truth about what it's like
Or how it really feels
But when you're out there for yourself
You can see the fear in others' eyes
You can feel their dread and pain
Because you feel the same.

Harriet Arthur (13)
Clayton Hall Business & Language College, Newcastle

War's Definition

We all know what war means,
Pure violence, no silence.
Eventually brings peace
A disagreement leading to a flood of blood
Letting all hell loose
Simply known as legal abuse
What we'd like to reduce.
Creating everlasting grief
For those whose sons are feeling no relief.
Surrounded by guns
Men risking lives
Leaving wives
Behind for the rights of their country.

Habiba Ahmed (12)
Clayton Hall Business & Language College, Newcastle

99

Seasons

December is here and here comes the snow
It will come for a couple of months then disappear and go
But not before it drizzles with snow
Which causes mayhem and leaves people low
Spring eventually comes around
Letting people see the green ground
The daisies are back and grass starts to grow
Letting the world again move and flow
April and May fly by
Before summer arrives with the warm blue sky
Children play and have fun in the sun
Before autumn comes and makes it run
The cold is back with its evil touch
Making people not do that much
We're then back to the beginning with that horrible fear
We are ready again for another long year.

Evie Lyons (13)
Clayton Hall Business & Language College, Newcastle

A Parrot I Would Be!

I am a parrot of rainbow colours
My crown of orange like the fruit
Upon a king, my crown would suit.
My beak is yellow and very bright
Some would say it shines at night
My wings are red
Magnificent when spread
My breast of blue
I'm very proud when seen by you.
My tail is apple green
The nicest tail you've ever seen.
My back of purple and feet of pink
I'm a parrot of rainbow colours
Don't you think!

Adam Shann (12)
Clayton Hall Business & Language College, Newcastle

Lamb To The Slaughter

All the hatred in the world
It was now my time to face
The military had gone to war
And they wanted me to fight
But I was only sixteen
They couldn't expect me to
Could they?

I gingerly walked off the aeroplane
Into my teenage deathbed.
As I looked around at the horror of a battlefield
Was I really ready for this?
I remembered my mother's last words to me,
'Be proud son, do your country well.'

I died that day from a gunshot wound through my chest
But I staggered on fighting for my country, 'Freedom is ours!'

Megan Allingham (12)
Clayton Hall Business & Language College, Newcastle

Shall I Compare You To A Rose

Shall I compare you to a rose
With your luscious red hair
Your sweet-smelling perfume
Even your sharp temper
But it's not that bad
Because you're my rose
And I shall not forget you
Even when it's raining
Because you don't stand out
Though you're still there
As you're so pretty
But you're still angry
But so sweet
Just like the time we had to meet.

Matt Stride (14)
Clayton Hall Business & Language College, Newcastle

101

Devil

The word 'Devil' makes me shiver
The blood-red, the horns and pitchfork
The thought of it makes me quiver
Don't turn and call him a dork.

If you wander the streets alone in the dark
He could hurt you in an instant
And you thought that you were scared of a shark
Killing you is his comparison of killing an ant.

You think that Jaws is scary
He's got corrupt members walking the streets
Watch who you insult or things could get hairy
So in the morning when you're eating your Shredded Wheat
Beware of the Devil
The word 'Devil' makes me shiver
Does it not you?

Will Fedoroff (12)
Clayton Hall Business & Language College, Newcastle

Death

Though it may come
It will never go
If the dead had a secret
No one would know.
Though it may hurt
You will never overcome
Even if your name is Bert
You may as well cry
It won't last for long
But just remember this
It won't bring them back to life
There's some other detail
I want to mention
Next time it could be you!

David Broadhurst (12)
Clayton Hall Business & Language College, Newcastle

A Lie Good Or Bad?

A lie is like a puzzle to me

L ike a lock without a key
I t could spare people's feelings
E ven though it leaves your own conscience reeling

G uilt becomes a brand on your face
O thers can detect this so you start to sweat and pace
O n and on this torment goes, with increasing fear of getting caught
D eceit can be good but only when silence is bought

O ver time these lies get distorted
R unning away like an alien transported

B e careful when you tell your next lie
A s a label will stay with you until you die
D o not repeat a mistake once made because a lie good or bad
  will never fade.

Emily Taylor (13)
Clayton Hall Business & Language College, Newcastle

Nature

Over the rivers, forests, mountains and seas
Nothing seems to amaze me
More than the tulips coming into bloom
And the golden sunrays in June
The leaves rustling in the trees
Growing and falling in the summer breeze.
With animals grazing everywhere
A happy atmosphere fills the air
But like everything things will begin to change
Sometimes for the better and sometimes for strange
Creatures will die as time flies
So they must make the most of their lives while they still can
For whatever spring, summer or winter brings
Nature will affect all living things.

Kellyanne Miller (13)
Clayton Hall Business & Language College, Newcastle

One Breath

Take a breath
Take it deep,
'Calm yourself,' the general says to me
Take your gun and count to three,
1 . . . 2 . . . 3

Gas mask on
Devastation, death and depression surrounds me
I haven't said goodbye, so many people I'll miss.

Screams, cries, blood everywhere,
I feel the mud, the squelch in my boots.

I feel vibration shaking underneath me
I feel my life flash before my eyes
The sounds of sirens deafen my ears.
A crash in front of me, it was astounding, the last thing I saw!

Chantelle Quinton (13)
Clayton Hall Business & Language College, Newcastle

What Is Love?

Love, a powerful word
Used lots of times.
Love makes people do crazy things.
Why was love invented?
To hurt people,
Make them sad or unhappy
Or make them happy?
Love can have its ups
And also its downs.
But the way people act with
Love can make a difference.
A big one in my opinion.
Love can make people lie and even cry
But why?

Georgia Wilkes (13)
Clayton Hall Business & Language College, Newcastle

Eternal

Many times I've dreamt of you
But you never did appear
To hold me close
And tell me you care.

Even when the sky darkens
For the last time
And the world we know is no more
My heart will still long for its other half.

Safely in your arms I wish to stay
For the rest of our days
And even when above
I know I've found my eternal love.

Demi Khetia (13)
Clayton Hall Business & Language College, Newcastle

Marriage

Love bears all things
Believes all things
Hopes all things
Endures all things.

It's the day of your wedding day
So perfect and fine
With all your friends around you to have a good time.

Love's like a roller coaster
You don't know what is coming next.
Marriage is a way of life
Marriage is so natural
Marriage is the better way for two to reach for Heaven.

Sarah Bithell (13)
Clayton Hall Business & Language College, Newcastle

Innocent

In World War II the average age of a soldier was twenty-six
In Vietnam it was nineteen, now in Afghanistan, it's just eighteen.
Innocent children going off to fight
But these children won't come back.

All around the noise of guns firing,
Bombs dropping, the stench of death lingers in the air.
Dead bodies line the streets and unhappiness is all around.

Innocent people get caught in the crossfire of disease and suffering.
People made homeless, children made orphans by a war that's
supposed to help.
Is war always bad or does some good come out of war?
Is war always necessary?

Meg Smith (12)
Clayton Hall Business & Language College, Newcastle

Victory

There they stood strong and proud
'Victory!' they shouted out loud.
It was done
The battle had been won.
Celebrations everywhere
Hands and banners waved in the air.
Outraged were the opposition
That they had been put in that position.
To lose is such an embarrassing thing
It rubs it in when the victors sing.
The smell of victory lingered in the air
The opposing team hung their heads in despair.

Jack Nixon-Davies (12)
Clayton Hall Business & Language College, Newcastle

Marriage

Once upon a time there was a marriage
In a golden white carriage.
As the marriage progressed
The girl fell into a lemon zest nest.
The boy was left in a mess
When he found the girl in the nest.
So as the day went on the girl and the boy were both in a mess
When they heard about the rest.
As the boy and girl struggled through the zest
They didn't want to be late for their test.
Plus with all the lemon zest
They were trying to look their best.

Layla Ayub (12)
Clayton Hall Business & Language College, Newcastle

Death

The long untold pain
With everyone pleading for help
What hundreds of people dreaded
Was just around the next corner
Lurking over the bloodshot fields
People lying dead!
Many pleading, begging for help
Hundreds of them, lying there
Death is horrible once
Death is terrible in tens
Death is horrific in hundreds
Death in thousands.

Reece Wright (12)
Clayton Hall Business & Language College, Newcastle

No One's Land

Smoke, smoke in the air
Blood and guts lying everywhere
Shells, shells, I hear Hell's bells
Screaming, yelling, no retreat
Were strong together, like a big band
Standing here on no-man's-land
The band is breaking, getting weak
The battle is losing, getting bleak
No chance to win
We're going to lose
The war is lost
This is the end.

Sam Booth (14)
Clayton Hall Business & Language College, Newcastle

A Shot

A shot is a shot to kill
No matter what the name, Henry, Bill or Phil.
A shot, is a shot with a bad intention
Just like it's a bad invention.

A shot, is a shot with a gun
Causes pain and is definitely not fun.
A shot is shot at war
And hurts a family at the core.
Pain and hurt, blood will splurt.

James Smith (13)
Clayton Hall Business & Language College, Newcastle

Why?

You march, you chant,
You laugh, why?

You dodge, you shoot,
You kill, you cry.

You live, you duck,
You dive, you lie.

You crawl, you crouch,
You fall, you die.

Jonathan Crick (13)
Clayton Hall Business & Language College, Newcastle

War Is Not Peaceful

We cover our ears to avoid the deafening sound
Of large guns firing left, right and all around.

I turn around to see men drop like flies down to the ground
Some men are discovered but some are never found.

Many families wondering, *will this war ever end?*
Lots are lost in the war, husband, son or a best friend.

Many men are lost in the troops they have to send
War is not a peaceful thing, although it's easy to pretend.

Jess Bates (12)
Clayton Hall Business & Language College, Newcastle

It's True

It's true I've got so much love for you.
It's true that you're the only one.
It's true that I adore you.
It's true you make me feel alive.
It's true that you make the day go by.
It's true you make me love you.

David Fox-Wells (14)
Clayton Hall Business & Language College, Newcastle

Death

Some people don't want to die
Some day their loved ones will cry
Death is a part of life
It could happen with a knife
Murder is one way, illness another
But one thing's for sure
Your family shares memories with each other.

Aaron Taft (12)
Clayton Hall Business & Language College, Newcastle

Black

Black
Not a friend or a foe
Not for happy, not for woe
Death, disaster, evil, doom
Things that go bump inside your room
But just because black can symbolise night
Doesn't mean you should throw insults at civil rights.

Andreas Welsh (12)
Clayton Hall Business & Language College, Newcastle

Heartbroken Poem

Sorrow and weakness
Is how I am feeling
Encouraged and being blessed
That is how I am healing.
For that one last chance I had
To spend with my loved one
Has gone, has passed, too bad.
I should've been holding on
And now I survive
Till this very moment
It was your love that kept me alive
It was your love that was dominant
But now that you are no longer here
My heart shall fade away
Oh how I wish you were near
And all will turn to grey
So once again I lay around
With a broken heart.
When I lay I didn't make a sound
So now I must start
The search for true love again
But I'm sure that won't happen
Until I find someone called Jamie Finnegan
Oh your name always had me laughing
And then the love I find
Will sure to fade away
Separate us like lemon and limes
And until this very day
It still is your love that keeps me alive
It still is your love that remains dominant
But now that you are no longer here
My heart shall fade away
Oh how I wish you were near
And all will turn to grey.

Daniella Evans (12)
Fairfax School, Sutton Coldfield

Black History Poem

Hello, my name is Sam
And my poem is about the story of black people long ago.
What happened back then was a sham
And I think everyone should know.

Kidnapped from the place they wanted to be
Taken off to a faraway land,
Oh but if only they could see
That their life here on in wasn't grand.

Squashed on a ship, chained up all day, life was dull,
Taken out once a day to do gym.
Thrown overboard if they weren't careful
As he fell I said, 'I knew him.'

Auctioned off to their doom
Where they would have to work hours on end.
Men in the fields, women in the posh rooms,
Here there were no rules to bend.

There was a fight between north and south
North for justice, south for slavery.
Every side gave each other mouth
The north won the civil war, blacks were free!

But that wasn't the end of the story
As hatred still roamed the Earth.
They had no time to bask in glory
As they were beaten and given hard work.

This continued for years and years
Something had to be done.
As people broke down in tears
Martin Luther king had his son.

This beautiful man changed everything
Gave them a future, some hope.
He was doing so well he could sing
Martin wouldn't get put down by the word 'Nope'.

He went against rivals and won
Everyone thought he was great.
But someone out there had a gun
Martin died April 4th, 1968.

This caused riots and havoc
At the outrage of this man's death hearts were torn.
But just a few years before his death
A man called Barack Obama was born.

He fought against John McCain
For the right to run the States.
John fought valiantly
But Barack won all the debates.

Now he is President of America, he won his game
It kind of proves
That black people are the same,
They lost a few battles but the war they certainly did not lose!

Sam Thompson (12)
Fairfax School, Sutton Coldfield

Mrs Bevan!

'Mrs Bevan! Mrs Bevan! I can't find my pen.'
'Come over here and get one then.'
'Mrs Bevan, I hurt my hand!'
'Don't be silly, stop messing around.'
'Mrs Bevan, Mrs Bevan, have you got a cat?'
'Be quiet, it's a test and stop doing that!'
'Mrs Bevan, Mrs Bevan, you're the best!'
'I know, I know, better than the rest!'

Sharmarni Brown (11)
Fairfax School, Sutton Coldfield

Seasons

Water so clear, ever so blue,
Can see your reflection and the sun too.
Flowers bloom colourful and bright,
To yellow to purple, what a beautiful sight.
Trees so tall, grass so green,
The greatest sight I have ever seen.

Clouds move into the light,
Until it's dark, until it's night.
Children sing and run around,
What a wonderful, a wonderful sound.
Sunset blends with the blue, blue skies,
That's where the real treasure lies.

Leaves start to fall on the soft, soft ground
Twirling, twirling and twirling around.
Midsummer skies form slowly in the air,
Gently overlapping the perfect pair.
Mountains shaded in brown and grey.
Sending a message, a message to say
Autumn is here and it's here to stay,
Feel the breeze as it grows and grows
Until it stops and everything goes.

White gentle snow falls on the ground
Covering the path without a sound.
Sky so white, up in the air
Gently falling, without a care.
Trees sway so gently
So this is what you will see
Cobwebs frozen in straight lines
All connecting to a street sign.

Kate Helen Orton (13)
Fairfax School, Sutton Coldfield

My Poem

Things that go together
Lavender and heather
Strawberries and cream
Chocolate ice cream
Black peppercorn
An elf and leprechaun
Things that go together
My father and mother
Bees and honey
Credit cards and money
Loans and debts
Dogs and vets
Sweet and treats
Pickled meats
Pick 'n' mix
Clowns and tricks
Sugar and spice
All things nice
Tin and foil
Vegetable oil
Things that go together
Never and forever
Dumb and clever
Onward never
Stories with a writer
Wrestles with a fighter
Day and night
Flying the kite
Things that go together.

Callum Flatley (12)
Fairfax School, Sutton Coldfield

115

Identity

Everyone has their own identity
Everyone has a background
The people with good economy
Make a happy sound.

But for some it's not the same
They live in poverty, sadness and pain
They get judged if they're different or quiet
People may even start a riot.

The aim of this poem is to get you to see
No one is the same as me
Ethnic cultures and religion too
They all make people like you.

Landscapes and climates make
A place to live and have a break
But for some small kids that's not true
Because of all the work they do.

They work and struggle day and night
Life for them is never right
Washing pans and scrubbing floors
Cutting their fingers when repairing doors.

This is what happens to children today
When they're stuck in poverty with no time to play
Don't you think this sounds really sad
Make a difference and get rid of the bad.

Joshua Boyce (12)
Fairfax School, Sutton Coldfield

Last Moments

The night dims on my face
The blood creeps down from my veins
I feel my energy leaking out of me
My soul will be long gone
My sanity is killing me softly as it drips away
Just like the present time, my last few minutes
Drip drop . . . tick-tock
Pulling me away, pulling me away.
You are no longer my dear life
Because you no longer matter to me
The light is fading
Voices are wailing
But I depart from this world
From this life and as always I know truly am
Lonely, dead, forgotten.

Elizabeth Pickering (13)
King Edward VI School, Lichfield

All In My Head

A massive fancy house
Not fit for a mouse
Just fit for a queen
So it's just fit for me!

A huge drive
A cinema inside
Not to hide
It's fit for a queen
So it's just fit for me!

A live band (JLS)
To play in the sand
In my garden.

It is fit for a queen
So it's just for me!

Simran Shergill (12)
Menzies High School Science College, West Bromwich

117

War

War causes pain
War causes misery
I see all of the dead bodies
Guns blazing
Bombs dropping
People screaming
People collapsing
War tears lives apart
Refugees walking
Dying
Running
Shelter is all they think of
War causes death
Emotion
Noise
Unknown enemies invading
Spreading like a virus inside a body
Slaves desperate
It's like the Holocaust all over again
War consumes life
Kids walking with no protection but a knife
War is insane.

James Joseph Michael Howell (11)
Menzies High School Science College, West Bromwich

Spooky Night

It was dark and spooky in the night
As the big bold moon was the only light
The bats were coming out to play
But the trees scared them away.

There was a spooky church nearby
And it nearly reached the dark sky
The wind whistled with owls too
As this poem scares me and you.

Aaron Woodard (12)
Menzies High School Science College, West Bromwich

Halo War

A grunt with a sticky grenade to his face
Him dying like that was a real disgrace
A banshee shooting a ravishing shot
But destroyed by the power that a Spartan laser got.

A brute killed Buck with a Gravy Hammer's force
He's deadest of the dead without any cures
A jackal with a sniper
Cried like a baby with a diaper
He was going to get hit
By a Spartan's super deadly fist.

A squad of banshees soon come down
To a man with a missile pod and a frown
He destroyed the three ships
Quick and accurate, like a whip

Soon goes down the final hunter
And the men return to a bunker
Even though they just won
The war has only just begun.

Tom Willetts (12)
Menzies High School Science College, West Bromwich

Winter

The darkest evening of the year
I slowly walk without any fear
On the ground
A sheet of white
And the reflection of my light.

The howling wind in my ear
The freezing snow falls near
It falls like glitter
Without a sound
As I slowly look around.

Ifzaa Hussain (12)
Menzies High School Science College, West Bromwich

119

Bad Day To The Beach

Along those sandy beaches
Many people lie
Looking up to the sky
Waiting for that bright sunlight.

The sea's moving wolfishly
Now it's calmed down
They all go to splash each other
Without making a frown.

Children building sandcastles
The sun has now disappeared
The seagulls no longer seen
So they all watch in fear.

The sky has now gone grey
So they all run to the hills
Watching the rain pour down
Without making a sound.

The day has now come to an end
So they all leave and pack
The others hold their sacks
On their firm cold backs.

Aysha Rai (11)
Menzies High School Science College, West Bromwich

A Cold Winter's Day

On this cold winter's day
I am going to play
In the snow and ice
I think it's really nice.

I get my gloves and hat
And move my pussycat
I am now really cold
I'm getting really old.

My body is freezing
Like an ice cube
I better keep warm
Or else I am doomed.

The snow is coming down
Really, really slow
I don't know
Where to go.

The cold air freezes me
I wish I was drinking a cup of tea
On this cold winter's day
I am going out to play.

Paul Roberts (12)
Menzies High School Science College, West Bromwich

The Tropical Jungle

As the leaves of the trees dance in the wind
The toucans start to fly
The frogs who are really green
Start to beam in the sunlight.
The snakes start hissing
Instead of kissing
Or are they?

When the breeze goes through the jungle
It seizes the crows
And as the sun shines upon
The trees start having fun
And the flowers have lots of powers.

Trust those in the jungle
There is no fear around
But when the tiger comes the whole thing falls apart
Now remember the tiger is looking around and when it comes just shout!

Rose Dhiman (11)
Menzies High School Science College, West Bromwich

In The Night

The day has passed, the sun is set,
And the stars are in the sky;
While the grass is wet
And through the air the bats are a-fly.

The fog is still and dark and deep
And on the hill the old room rests;
The birds soon find their nests
And the lambs now go to sleep.

And through the fields both dark and deep
Through the grass the wind creeps;
All of the children should be resting their heads
So go to sleep in your sweet beds.

Tian Melia (12)
Menzies High School Science College, West Bromwich

The Tree

The tree in Japan
People think it's crying
It is crying
You can see a tear.

It is crying because of fear
Each day facial images appear
Until one day it comes to life
But it is still crying.

Instead of fear it cries for joy
But suddenly the tree turns to a normal tree
It never cries
And never dies
It just stays in one place
And never again it has a face.

Viraj Patel (12)
Menzies High School Science College, West Bromwich

The Wilderness

Past the ditch that protects Varrock
And over the tremendous rock
Revenant creatures hide in the shadows
And overgrown rats break through rain windows
Bandits and rogues set up camp there
Also it contains a King Black Dragon's lair

People who enter are never seen again
The ground is covered in broken armour and chain
Creatures from Hell lurk around too
Lesser and greater demons, hell-hounds and creatures of goo
Lava possess most of the ground
When grizzly bears, dark unicorns and zombies hear a sound
They'll attack fiercely with no hesitation
The wilderness would be danger to any nation!

Dale Britton (11)
Menzies High School Science College, West Bromwich

123

The Shopping Mall

In the shopping mall
There's a massive shoe mall
It's a girl's delight
I think I'll go shopping tonight.

There's clothes shops
And shoe shops
Old shops
And new shops.

Shopping is just great
I hope I'm not too late
To buy my favourite things
Maybe even a diamond ring.

Georgina Amy Corbett (11)
Menzies High School Science College, West Bromwich

The Dark Night

The ground wet with dew
The sky scattered with stars
The night is dry
'So beautiful,' I cry.

The trees madly blown
By the ferocious wind
The water level low
In the lovely stream.

The owl has awoken now
Though I don't know how
Hooting away
Asleep in the day.

Tamara Davies (11)
Menzies High School Science College, West Bromwich

The Beach

The seagulls go by
While the crabs say hi
The sun goes down
And the sand starts to frown.

People come every day
Even in May
They play netball
The best one is very tall.

The shells are happy to be collected
Even though only some are selected
The beach is a great place to be
It is a good sight to see.

John Marks (12)
Menzies High School Science College, West Bromwich

The Unusual Yet Creepy House

Along the corridor you go
All the same dull colours in a row
The floor is wobbly
And the door is crooked
People don't dare to go there
Not even one little stare.

Up the stairs you go
The stairs seem to grow
The first door on the left
Had a massive hole as if this house had a theft
Moving on to the end of the corridor
There doesn't seem to be a path anymore.

Shelby Agger (12)
Menzies High School Science College, West Bromwich

War Is Bad

There are bullet holes everywhere
A soldier jumps out and gives you a scare
It is very dirty and muddy
All the buildings are very cruddy
It's a very long journey back
And all the jeeps go off track.

They hate it so much
They're against the Dutch
They wish they could go home to their wife
But instead they get stabbed with a knife
It smells really bad
He is in a war just like his dad.

Jacob Spray (12)
Menzies High School Science College, West Bromwich

A Small War

A very, very wet war
Death and violence that's what they saw
A deathly field held
Someone fighting with a shield
A muddy battle
A few dead cattle

It was like a world war
That one man saw
The lightning struck
They began to fight
Poppies were caught
In memory of those who fought.

Sunish Patel (12)
Menzies High School Science College, West Bromwich

The Abandoned House

As the wind whistles
Like a moaning ghost
The weeds blow
Fairly close.

A whirling wind of leaves form
As they fall off the trees
Onto the floor.

The Earth blows around the windows
Of the abandoned house.
The door has been blown off
By an angry wind.

Cheryl Smith (12)
Menzies High School Science College, West Bromwich

The Rat

The cat chased the rat like it was a piece of meat
It looked so tasty and delicious
As the rat ran away it squeaked its voice
It sounded as light as a penny dropping on the floor
How would you feel if you were being chased?
The cat's teeth were as sharp as a knife blade
It was dribbling and staring
The rat wanted to run but was stuck in a corner
It was trapped and the car jumped towards it
It felt as frightened as lightning.

Sophie Allsop (11)
Menzies High School Science College, West Bromwich

Silent Is The Night

Above the silence; the sky bled at seams,
As the Starry God melts; lemon ice cream
On top of the hot cookie horizon; failing,
Fading, fringing existence. Then it's gone and there is just:
                              Us.

Silent is the night, all I feel is Her.
Swelling emotion; Her eyes; two heavenly burning sapphires
Look through mine; and fair angels, bearing Cupid's arrow, fly into
my soul;
Fair wings softly swooping beautifully, as they stir soul's dull waters.

Through the tranquil night, a swift slight wind silently stirs creating
whispers of Her hair
Upon the gracious air. Beautiful …

Her angular face emits a cerise curve which shines slicing Dusk.
Her eyes still stand;
Amazing, as Moon doth dutifully draw his mystical blade - in hand -,
In salute of Her glory!

Her smooth skin blesses mine with its grace;
Coolness seeping through to me. I feel strangely . . . safe.
Enchanted Our lips do linger, in blissful connection
As Our arms hold each other; in affection
Her body radiates beauty.
                    I feel Her breathing.
                                        Her heartbeat.
                                                        Her love.

Silent is the night …

Heerunpal Gill (14)
Queen Mary's Grammar School, Walsall

128

The Darkness And The Moon

The moon; a glistening sphere
Its exquisite, ethereal light
But as it powers through the cloudless sky
Out comes the black twilight . . .

Darkness rages viciously,
A relentless, impenetrable force.
The master of black and night itself
A dark power source.

The graceful and serene moon
Comes out an astounding sight!
Her bright and dazzling beauty
Darkness looks at her in spite.

The roaring winds stand aside
For magnificent black and white!
But vision, obscured by the stillness of the sky,
It is truly an invisible fight . . .

But the coming of the end is soon,
The end of the darkness and the moon . . .

However the day will finish
And they will stand side by side
Looking at each other in malice
So again, they will rise.

Namir Rahim Chowdhury (12)
Queen Mary's Grammar School, Walsall

They, The Dark-Hearted Sparks

Clearly filled with energy. Nothing but bliss
Could step into their minds. Learning, novel and chaste.
Like the winds of the seas, nothing could replace.
But all of that was when the world was free,
Now the monster has trapped and hidden the key.
It was they, the dark-hearted sparks, surrounded by rage.

They were the outcome of selfish pleasure,
Coming from those who knew not of this treasure.
Their life started off as a consequence
Rather than the desire and adore we received.
When they cried their first cry, it echoed softly
Into a mist in which they were ever lost.
Yes they, the dark-hearted sparks, surrounded by rage.

With no hope of escape, something never seen.
Every day would be the start of agony;
Dawn to dusk, an old forced independence.
Hungry and weak they would sit in the corner
Waiting for God to show His mercy
But when it became clear nothing would change
They would stand and find what dire filth was left.
No flavour, no love, nothing but lament.
Yes they, the dark-hearted sparks, surrounded by rage.

Yes, when our childhood stood upon us
We shone, and twinkled bright. With affectionate fuss,
Spoiled and nurtured with utmost worth,
Our minds were sparkling, as stars newly born.
Free of concern and the wicked of this doleful planet
But they, the dark-hearted sparks, were surrounded by rage.

There were always the lonely ones, and the quiet,
With blackened hearts and no sight for good.
The scars of their pains reflected on their eyes
And on their backs, the wounds awarded by their owners.
Forlorn, forgotten. Just another day.
Disposed, unwanted. Their conscience always grey.
They, the dark-hearted sparks, surrounded by rage.

Unlike us, the lucky, they will always hold strife.
They were meant to be sparks of purity and life,
But the monsters encaged them, and burned their hope
With no clemency. Their eyes were red
Brows folded, monsters all over; ready to strike.
Their eyes were closed, bruises, cuts and ache all over; ready to die
Will you save them, or leave them to suffer?
Will you save them and free them from the cage?
They, the dark-hearted sparks, surrounded by rage.

Sabeeh Syed (16)
Queen Mary's Grammar School, Walsall

The Monsters Under My Bed

One thing my big brother said,
'Watch your back for the monsters under your bed!'
I thought he was just playing with my head
But the words kept filling me with dread.

I thought, I'll be okay if I keep on the light
And not be subject to the spine-chilling sight.
Surely that must bring the biggest fright!
Alas, the monster still crept up on me in the night.

Then during that night, while my mind was clean
I felt hot breath, made of steam,
I knew it was a monster, scary and mean
And I gave a piercing scream.

So do not mess with a monster with eyes of lead
At that moment I knew I was going to be dead.
As he, with his bony hands, ripped off my head
I knew this was the monster from under my bed.

James Walkerdine (11)
Queen Mary's Grammar School, Walsall

O Feathery Feddle

If you ever go down main road
They will tell you of a boy named Feddle McToad
This is how the tale goes

Old Feddle ate lots of chicken
Monday was chicken day
Tuesday was turkey day
Wednesday was hen day
Thursday was goose day
Friday was cockerel day
Saturday was duck day
Finally Sunday was rest day

One day he's plump
The next he was a great big lump!
Then his mother said, 'Eat too much chicken and you will turn into
one!'

Monday his mouth turned into a beak
Tuesday he grew a tail . . . he even let off a wail
Wednesday his feet turned into talons
Thursday his skin turned to feathers, he even went to different salons
Friday he took a chicken shape with the backside curling along to his
nape
Saturday he was crying, 'Help, help, help!' Soon it was *cluck, cluck,
cluck!*
Sunday he was dead.

Sukhjeevan Singh Dhillon (11)
Queen Mary's Grammar School, Walsall

Short Lived

Sixteen and ignorant
Looking for adventure
I told a lie
I joined the army.
A costly decision.

At camp I made friends
I was trained well
I was given a rifle
With a bayonet on the end
I stuck it in a straw dummy, in training.

Thursday 12th, the day of reckoning
'Twas a gloomy day
Straight into combat
I killed my first Boche
A bayonet into flesh and blood,
I survived the first day.

Friday 13th, unlucky for some,
A hectic night with bloodshed
A miserable night for my friend and I.

Then there he was,
Death,
In the shape of a grenade.

Nikhel Chhiba (13)
Queen Mary's Grammar School, Walsall

A Cruel World

People screaming! Children crying!
The rising tide comes in along with the hordes of dead bodies
The ground vibrates with the blooded sand rippling . . .

A lone tiger stares at the natural disaster of the cruel world
His eyes obsolete, his mouth dry
Roaring for food, it trembles along
His feet sore, ruined by rubble
He prances on the dry ground
Surrounded by debris, not mentioning the lifeless bodies

Astounded, the survivors run
He means no harm, he is searching for food
The barren lands utterly love him
He is living a hell.

Dilan Patel (11)
Queen Mary's Grammar School, Walsall

My Little Brother

My little brother is only two
But he's cool and he's funny
And he loves my shoes.

He speaks a little bit
But he laughs a lot.
Sometimes he's a pain
But I don't see why not.

He's only a baby
But he understands
Our love for each other
Is impeccably grand.

I love my little brother
He's a darling, a saint.
So here's to my brother
The everlasting great!

Charlotte Hill (13)
St Dominic's School, Brewood

I Know The Truth - Do You?

Every punch I receive, will bound upon my arm.
A brutal blue bruise,
My father is a bull, disguised as a harmless puppy.
But I know the truth.

They hold my hand,
Wish me luck on my first day of school.
I pray it would stay like this forever
But I know the truth.

The pain striking my legs,
The spit of abuse showering down on me,
That feeling of loneliness.
But only I will ever know the truth.

Maneshia Johal (14)
St Dominic's School, Brewood

Snow

Snow is falling on the ground
Children playing, having fun.
Slippy slush, so steady steps
Thermal socks, slippery slopes.
Icy roads, careful modes.

Kelly Anne Westwood (12)
St Dominic's School, Brewood

Silent
(Inspired by 'A Poem to be Spoken Silently' by Pie Corbett)

It was so quiet that
I could hear the clouds
Singing a lullaby to the rainbow.

It was so still that
I could feel the Earth's crust
Getting hotter and hotter.

It was so quiet that
I could hear a waterfall
Evaporating into thin air.

It was so still that
I could feel the crunch
As a fairy bit into her abracadabra cherry pie.

It was so silent that
I could hear the moon
Turn off its lights as it went to sleep.

It was so tranquil that
I could feel my shadow
Moving without me.

It was so quiet that
I could hear the stars playing
Their flutes on planet Neptune.

Emma Sans (12)
St Dominic's School, Brewood

Lycans

The full moon, you may just think of it like a never-ending cycle
But for me it's different.
It changes me from girl to beast
A change that I can't stop.

I look at the full moon and shudder,
I fall to my knees and feel the change rippling through my body.
I close my eyes and let the transformation take place.

I open my eyes and see the night in new eyes
And feel my hind legs eager to move,
Eager to dig my claws into the ground,
Eager to run!

I run through the forests pushing myself to the limit
I stop and sniff the air, I knew they would find me, they always do.
I step out onto the clearing and stare at the pack, my family.

I make my mark on the pack and show my respect to the alphas
I turn towards the forest and howl and the howls increase like a
chorus of rain.

The hunt has begun!
I see a shadow out of the corner of my eyes and run.
I chase the prey through the forest and smell the fear seeping out of
the prey in waves
I jump on its back and drag it to the ground.
I wait for the alphas to make the kill.
My hunger growling at the wait and my heart beats wildly and I make
the kill.
I look around and run, I can never show my face again.

Cleopatra Darwish (12)
St Dominic's School, Brewood

137

Late

I'm late, late, late
For a very important date.
I'll hop, zoom and fly
Right through the sky.

I'm late, late, late
To go and see my mate.
I've hopped, zoomed, flew and I've landed,
I'm standing here on a pier.

I'm late, late, late
To go and see Kate.
I've hopped, zoomed, flew and I've landed
I'm standing here
On a pier.
She's over there,
Do you think she will care?
She looks quite mad
Which makes me sad.
All because I was
Late, late, late
For a very important date
To go and see my mate
Whose name is Kate.

Hannah-Mae Prodger (12)
St Dominic's School, Brewood

Pyjamas

Did you know pyjamas are a serious thing?
Everyone wears them, even the king.
Really old people wear them too,
Cows have some that say 'Moo!'

When you go to the pyjama temple and you hear the pyjama song
You should know that it's time to sing the pyjama song.

'Pyjamas, pyjamas
Everyone has pyjamas
Pyjamas, pyjamas
You have to have some too.'

In the pyjama temple they pray to a pyjama god
Then they have to go to sleep in a pyjama pod.
You know there's a pyjama school
Me and my pyjamas went there and it's so cool.
In the school they have a lesson all about sleeping
Instead of the head teacher they have a pyjama king!
His name is Pyjama Pete
I wanted to go meet and greet.
I thought about changing into my best pyjamas
I got them from the Bahamas
I hope it's not a disaster.

Reece Billen (11)
St Dominic's School, Brewood

Rush

Come on everybody
Time to get up,
Our plane will be leaving this morning for Crete
No later than 10 o'clock.

Those jeans are ripped and dirty
Put on another pair,
Now hurry up, pick up the pace
Don't just stand and stare!

Don't shovel down your breakfast
Savour every bite,
Will you or your brother get the phone?
Please don't start to fight.

The taxi will be late today
Tell your dad we need his car
What do you mean it's at the garage?
OK, call your grandad, there's a star.

Put on your seat belts everyone
Let's do a check, don't make a sound,
Passport, tickets, money, make-up . . .
Stop! Turn around!

Megan Carter (12)
St Dominic's School, Brewood

My Musical Hamster

I love hamsters
Hamsters are cute
But my hamster's special
He plays the flute!

He has a special tune
On his special red flute
And his special tune goes
Toot, toot, toot!

Drum, dum, dum
Go the drums that he plays
And when he's feeling happy
To the music he will sway!

I bought him little jazz shoes
To fit his little feet
So now when he goes dancing
He can tap to the beat!

I love my hamster
And my hamster loves me
And every time I see him
We catch up with cups of tea.

Ella Molin (12)
St Dominic's School, Brewood

Shopping!

Shop, shop, shop, shop till I drop,
Spend, spend, spend, no need to lend,
I have my plastic and that's just fantastic.

Up and down escalators at the mall
Looking for a dress to wear at the ball
Black, white, gold, silver, blue
Oh my, what to do?

Topshop, New Look, River Island and Next
Warehouse, Jaegar, Henleys and Mex
Retail therapy is what I need
A way to unwind and satisfaction guaranteed.

Going out excited!
Everyone's on a high
Coming home exhausted
Oh my, oh my.
My desire's fulfilled
I can relax,
Coming home to a coffee
Living life to the max!

Elisha Sharma (14)
St Dominic's School, Brewood

Naughty Rabbits

The morning of a new day
Alfie and Freddie ready to play
Getting their food ready to eat
Carrots, lettuce, toast and hay
Open the door of the wooden hutch
Their faces full of joy.

The pitter-patter of their fluffy paws
Noses poking through the bars
Getting up on their hind legs ready to escape
Waiting, waiting, waiting for that moment.

Katie Ann Beck (12)
St Dominic's School, Brewood

Holiday

That holiday was great
Perhaps we should go again
Next time bring a mate
No, that would be a pain
Maybe to Spain
To Italy
That's lame.

Okay, okay, to Italy we fly
You may take off your seatbelt
Yeah, we are so high
Hope you brought the water or you and I will melt!

Bang! Smash! Wallop! Plop!
What in the world,
Did we drop?
No, don't worry the plane just curled
You'll be okay once we have . . .
Argh!

Jessica Mae Holmes (12)
St Dominic's School, Brewood

Cricket Game

I am waiting in the locker room
Waiting for my time to shine.
My heart is beating faster and faster
I have to clear my mind.
Looking out of the window
Looking into the batter's eyes
'I see,' she says
'You're running out of time.'
I pick up my helmet, my bat and my gloves,
I walk out the door with a push and a pull.
The bowler bowls the ball down fast
Wicket, catch, what will it be?
Instead the bowler screams as she breaks her knee!

Emma Hudson (11)
St Dominic's School, Brewood

143

The Man Next Door

My brother and I do the paper round for the street,
Early in the morning with no time to sleep.
With heavy bags for only five pounds a week
But get lots and lots of lovely treats.

It takes us an hour to do it all
Running around like headless fools
Until we reach the man next door,
The giant who has an almighty roar!

We leave his papers on the floor
So he doesn't see us walking past his door.
Until the next day comes to do it again
To run along like we are playing a game.

But I won't do that any longer
Run away, I will be stronger.
Stand there till he opens the door,
Then say, 'Hello, I live next door.'

Bethany Clansey (12)
St Dominic's School, Brewood

My Dances

Ballet
Pull up your tights
Put on your shoes
On goes your leotard
Ready for lesson
Skips and bar
Pirouette and plie
Now to the lesson to dance, dance, dance.

Jazz
I walk into the lesson five minutes late
There stands a teacher waiting to teach
I hop and I skip and I jump and I turn
All the way to the end of the lesson!

Bethanie Grace Morris (11)
St Dominic's School, Brewood

144

My Cat

My cat is a tabby cat
Tilly is her name
She plays with mice
It's her favourite game.

She's sleek and sly
And loves to get muddy.
Bites a lot
And annoys me when I study.

She is a sleepy cat
Sleeps in the day.
Until I feed her
Then she wants to play.

She sits by the fire
And has a big yawn.
She falls into a deep sleep
All cosy and warm.

Emily Heath (11)
St Dominic's School, Brewood

Milk

Milk is nice.
Milk is sweet.
Milk is healthy for your bones and teeth.

I like milk in my tea.
I like milk as a drink.
I like milk in my cereal.

Lovely milk, cold and fresh.
Lovely milk, creamy and hot.
Lovely milk, white and sweet.

Keep milk in my fridge,
Kick start to the day,
Keeps people with strong bones.

Sabrina Rohail Aslam (12)
St Dominic's School, Brewood

The Locker Room

The locker room is very small,
We couldn't lose a bouncy ball.
The teachers think it's all okay
When we get squished every day.

It's break time now, we're going to play,
Come on Emma, let's get away -
From the locker room, it's all packed now,
Full of pupils having a row.

Ding-dong, oh no, not again,
Here comes the stampede, prepare for pain.
It's lunchtime now, it's roast today,
Come on now, move out my way.

The end of the day has arrived at last,
Oh no, now it's the locker room dash.
Pushing and shoving, get out of my way,
I need to get home now; it's that time of day.

Annie-Rose Griffiths (11)
St Dominic's School, Brewood

Cheese

Cheese is great and full of delicious flavours
It's in lots of foods starting with Quavers.
Cheese comes in different shapes and sizes
And at a tombola it's used in all different prizes.

Cheese, my favourite would probably be
Cheddar or Edam and definitely Dairylea.
Cheese strings, cheesecake but which is the best?
Cheese in a can is better that the rest.

Cheese can be yellow, blue or red
I like to dream of cheese when I'm in my bed.
Cheese can smell like stilton which I cannot stand
Cheese is not for everyone but I just think it's grand.

Emily Round (11)
St Dominic's School, Brewood

The Perfect Night

Flames dancing in the fire,
Everyone stood near to get warm
Fireworks rose again and again
Everyone went, 'Aah' when they rose again.

All different colours high up in the sky
All making beautiful swirls and shapes in the sky.

After they had ended
Everyone sat around the fire
Everyone having a laugh
Smiling and having a good time.

When the night came to an end
The place grew quiet
The wind grew calm
And the children's voices grew tired
The perfect night to end a perfect day.

Ellena Thomas (13)
St Dominic's School, Brewood

I Can't Think Of Anything To Write

I can't think of anything to write
It's giving me a bit of a fright.
What to do, I really don't know
So please help this writer's block go.

I can't think of anything to do
Well, do you? I am getting rather irritated
So help me get out of this state.

I can't think of anything to put
I have a bad feeling in my gut.
Please will you help me?
I'm feeling rather empty.

I can't think of anything to write
So I'm in a bit of a fright.

Sarah Cowling (13)
St Dominic's School, Brewood

147

Evil Brothers And Sisters

Brothers and sisters are evil,
Mean and manky as well.
They torture and trick you
And constantly kick you,
But when you fight back they just yell!

We fight in the morning whilst cleaning our teeth,
At lunchtime we fall out again.
When teatime arrives, Mum, head in hands, sighs,
'Will you ever get on then?'

Don't you just hate it
When they tell tales and invent things
When you haven't done anything at all?
They're a pain in the neck!
But hang on a sec,
They're my brothers and sisters after all!

Poppy Thompson (11)
St Dominic's School, Brewood

The Life Of A Fish Like Me

I am a fish
Swimming in the sea.
I swim all day
Busy as a bee.
As I swim along
I meet my best friend Smee.
We go to the café
To have some seaweed tea.
After that
We're all full of glee.
And that is the life
Of a fish like me.

Megan Watson (12)
St Dominic's School, Brewood

Moonshine

I hear his hooves banging impatiently at the door.
He's telling me his food's gone and he needs more.
I run through the lush, green paddock and I see him pacing,
My little sister is behind me, first she walks then she starts racing.
He is black, as black as night, as graceful as a soaring kite.
He loves to gallop; he's as fast as lightning.
He wouldn't hurt a fly, in fact, he finds thunder frightening.
He may be black but he shines like the moon.
I let him out and I say, 'See you soon.'
He rears up then comes crashing down, splitting the Earth into two.
In the moonlight he glistens the darkest dark blue.
His name is Moonshine and Moonshine is mine!

Caitlin Beaumont (12)
St Dominic's School, Brewood

My Dog, Mollie

M y dog Mollie
Y elps, yowls and yaps

D oes love to swim
O verexcited, like an exploding can of soda
G oes mad when she sees a cat

M oves like a fish in the water
O bviously my favourite
L oyal and loving, she's all these things
L oopy Labrador
I ntuitive that's her
E verlasting best friend.

Katherine Rigg (13)
St Dominic's School, Brewood

149

The Reality Of War

Running towards the enemy,
Many old friends by my side.
But after just a few metres
Many have already died.

The rattle of a machine gun
Deadly bullets arch through the air.
But even with all this danger
There's no time to waste taking care.

I look at the men around me;
Dead eyes with no laughter or smile
Resigned to the fact that as they charge
They are running on their green mile.

Although I'm armed with grenades
And hold a pistol in my hand,
As I stand there I realise
I'm making my last stand.

A sudden explosion shakes me
Followed by the sound of a gun.
I hear the screams of the wounded
And I know the bomb's work is done.

The crack as I shoot my pistol
The thunder as they return fire.
We're trapped in a deadly stalemate
Waiting for the enemy to tire.

Suddenly under my feet
An enemy grenade blew
And as I lie there dying
I turn off the PlayStation 2.

Joe Knapper (14)
St Joseph's College, Stoke-on-Trent

Can You Imagine?

Can you imagine
A world without
War
Pain
Danger
Guns and
World poverty?

Can you imagine
A world with
War
Pain
Danger
Guns and
World poverty?

Can you imagine
If you were in the Holocaust
How would you feel?
Petrified
Worried
Would you survive?

Can you imagine
If you met Hitler
What would you do?
Attack him or
Back away from him?
Try to kill him or
Beg for your freedom?
Beg him to stop this rage
Against the Jews?

Philipp Woodward (12)
St Joseph's College, Stoke-on-Trent

A Holiday To Remember

A free holiday
How nice
We pack our bags
We leave tonight
We are taken to our bus
Looks like a pig sty
We whimper in
Something's up
The doors close
No windows
Five minutes in silence
Doors open.

Confusion strikes
In lines
People sent to shower
No one comes back
I'm next
Legs thrash
Head spins
Dragged off
Fight them
Get overpowered
Scream for help
No one comes
Dropped into shower
Fall asleep
Never awake.

James Morris (12)
St Joseph's College, Stoke-on-Trent

Untitled

A man fires a rifle for many years
No matter what he does with his hands
His hands will always remember the rifle.

Philip Watson (13)
St Joseph's College, Stoke-on-Trent

My Fairy Tale

One late night
In my dreams
I saw my love
Or so it seems.

He smiled at me
And said hello.
In a handsome voice
Of a fairy tale I know.

My cheeks blushed pink
I had to blink
When I arose,
I had to think
He was gone
Into thin air.
How I adored
His shiny hair.

His dark blue eyes
His faded smile
I looked around
For a while.
I never even knew his name
I hope I see my prince again.

Alexandra Horton (12)
St Joseph's College, Stoke-on-Trent

Can You Imagine . . . Death Is Music

The thick green fog weaving in and out of the pipes and organs
Deadly music to the ear, screeching, singing.
This was it, the war between us and it.
It hides in the cracks and gaps, listening, waiting.

Suddenly it attacks moving faster than light
Like a deadly Ferrari speeding round the death track.
There's only one word that comes to my mind, 'Death.'

Lauren Selby (13)
St Joseph's College, Stoke-on-Trent

153

Romeo And Juliet

Someone once told me
That love at first sight
Is nothing but lust
And ends in a fight

I always believed them
But I'll never forget
The day in English
When we watched Romeo and Juliet.

Because for once it seemed possible
To find your soulmate
The first time you see them
You know that it's fate

They would die for each other
They'd do anything at all
It's mutual love
Together they would fall

I know I'm young
And for me that's fine
I have my whole life
To find someone to be mine.

Lydia-Rose Phillips (14)
St Joseph's College, Stoke-on-Trent

Holocaust

H elp
O ur
L eaders
O ur
C ountry
A ttempts
U nless
S oldiers
T ry.

Jason Dunn (12)
St Joseph's College, Stoke-on-Trent

154

The Sea And The Waves Rolling Into Caves

The blue crystal sea
With its waves rolling free.

Like a bird in the sky
With its waves rolling high.

Like a magical stone
Its waves shatter bone.

Like a rag in the night
The waves start to fight.

Like a magical flower
Its waves have great power.

A sea that can soothe
Its waves slow their move.

In the final hour
The waves start to cower.

It's finally calm
The waves don't cause harm.

The blue crystal sea
With its waves rolling free.

Albert Joynson (13)
St Joseph's College, Stoke-on-Trent

Holocaust

H orrific - causing horror
O n your own
L iving with the
O ncoming death
C an you imagine
A ir polluted
U nbearable - not to be endured
S howers of gas
T ime to say farewell.

Sophie Berger (13)
St Joseph's College, Stoke-on-Trent

Would You Go To War?

Would you go to war
And fight for your country
Risk your life, die a hero?

Be brave, have no fear
Dodge bombs
Guide choking, dying soldiers,
Screaming and shouting like children in agony
Fighting for life!

Confused, tortured, beaten and scared,
Think of the helpless children,
Those in need of care
All of their dreams, gone! Covered in fantasy.

Gas attack, gas attack,
Run for your life,
Don't let it reach you,
And eat you alive.

Would you go to war
And fight for your country
Risk your life, die a hero?

Rosina Canonaco (12)
St Joseph's College, Stoke-on-Trent

Holocaust Memorial Poem

Can you imagine
A world of pain?
Watching your peers dying,
Dying for your help.
But you are too late!
As he choked like a smoker
He dropped to the muddy, decaying ground . . .
Dead!
Please remember, please don't forget
The 27th January, the day that doom met.

Alesi Steel (13)
St Joseph's College, Stoke-on-Trent

156

The Best Game Ever - Well Maybe Next Year Then . . .

We're going to Wembley
Of course we will win
Stoke are going to Wembley
I'm going with my mate Fin
We're going to Wembley
We are gonna take our seat in a min
Stoke are going to Wembley.

The FA Cup is the best
Us and United are the last two left
The next ninety minutes are gonna be a test.

Stoke are playing at Wembley
Fuller scores to put us ahead
Stoke are playing at Wembley
'Why, why Delilah?' rings from 40,000 heads.
Stoke fans are singing in Wembley
I won't forget this when I go to bed
Stoke win the FA Cup in Wembley
This was the greatest game for all
White and red.

William Bonsmann (14)
St Joseph's College, Stoke-on-Trent

Bombs Of Death

Can you imagine a world with
War, discrimination, pain, danger,
Torture and suffering?

Could you
Fight for your country,
Kill a city of civilians
And die for your country?

Would you
Discriminate, torture innocent people
And drop the bomb of death?

Sam Clarke (12)
St Joseph's College, Stoke-on-Trent

Can You Imagine?

Can you imagine
Guns, guns everywhere
Grenades and bullets flying through the air
Like fireworks going pop, crackle and bang?
Blood everywhere,
Soldiers being shot right in the heart dropping to the ground
Like hail on a bad winter's day.
Their pride and joy getting less and less
To save their Queen and country
From all this stress.
Coffins roll by, increasing more each day.
A soldier dies for all of us
They were fit but healthy before they were hurt
Their lives cut short
With much more to see.
So, can you imagine this awful time
And your friend being killed right by your side?
So, on the 27th January every year we take time to remember
Holocaust Memorial Day.

Jemma Rowe (13)
St Joseph's College, Stoke-on-Trent

The End!

If you could hear the screaming men
You would be terrified of big old Sam!
Gosh, he is a one with his little brother Ben
The blood drips down their face like jam.

His wild heart beats with painful sobs
His clenched hands try to carry on.
His aching jaws grip a hot parched tongue
His wide eyes unconsciously!

He cannot shriek
Saliva drips down his shapeless clothes
I saw him stab and stab again.

Lucy Prall (13)
St Joseph's College, Stoke-on-Trent

The Match

Me and my mates
Set off for the match
To see our team playing
In the top flight.
We all sit down
With our pies and Coke
And to our delight
They ain't playing their best bloke.
Then the ref blows the whistle
The cans in the bin
And after five minutes
Young Jonny bangs one in.
With the songs and the aggro
It's nearly ninety minutes
But I just don't want to go
But at least we won the match three-nil.
We'll just have to add the next game to the bill.
But all in all we had some fun
I hope next week we can say we've just won!

Sheldon Connell (14)
St Joseph's College, Stoke-on-Trent

In The Trenches

The bullets are blazing above my head
We never get the chance to go to bed.
We are in the trenches, tired and sleepy,
All the mud makes it very slippy.
The sound of death all around me,
I wish I was at home having my tea.
Bombs being dropped from the sky above,
You have to learn war's not love.
Then the gas comes and I hit the floor
I soon realise my life's no more.

Harry Lakin (13)
St Joseph's College, Stoke-on-Trent

159

Marching

Marching,
Proud or ashamed?
Proud - you're an individual,
It was your decision,
You could be saving your family.
Ashamed - you're independent,
Fighting the enemy,
The enemy who had the power, greed and selfishness to declare war.
Then you think . . .
You're just one of those men who could die fighting.
You're just one of those who every now and then have tears welling up
So that it just blurs your eyes.
You're like another book with its own story
But now it's a new chapter, a fresh page
March,
Proud . . . ashamed.

Isabella Frederick (12)
St Joseph's College, Stoke-on-Trent

Devil's Slaves!

They're born again, risen from the grave,
They're back for revenge - the Devil's slave.
Eyes glazed over with fury and lust,
Deformed, dripping flesh formed from earth and dust.

Feeling deranged and confused, I stagger on
Their mumbles burn my ears, until I think they are gone.
But lurking in the darkest depth of the night
The bloodthirsty souls with their eyes ghostly white.

They pierce your throat and drain all the life
Until your heart is as cold and sharp as a knife.
There's no hope in the world, no chance to survive
In that abyss of Hell, no one will revive!

Esther Greene (13)
St Joseph's College, Stoke-on-Trent

Random Animal Poem

Birds fly high
High in the sky
Make nests in trees
For their little fleas.

Hedgehogs walk
But sadly don't talk.
They are very spiny
And really are tiny.

Fish swim lots
And have no spots
They live in the water
With not that much torture.

A tortoise is slow
Fast, no, no, no.
They aren't very savage
But eat lots of cabbage.

Daniel Ratcliffe (13)
St Joseph's College, Stoke-on-Trent

Fresh And New

You are a spring day
All fresh and new.
You are bright and strong
Just like the sun.
But then spring changes to summer,
Summer to autumn,
Autumn to winter.
It takes a whole year
To get back to the start.
But with you
You're always fresh and new.
That is what I have,
Endless love for you.

Alannah Greenway (13)
St Joseph's College, Stoke-on-Trent

What Am I?

I'm not a laptop
I'm not a phone
So keep on guessing
And do not moan.

You press my only button
And slide me to unlock
You play with all my widgets
And plug me in my dock.

So listen to my music
And play all of my games
Do you know what I am yet?
I have only one name.

You've guessed it, I'm an iPod
And I'm yours to keep forever.
As updates are available
Forever, and ever and ever!

Joseph Federici (12)
St Joseph's College, Stoke-on-Trent

My Stupid Dog

My dog is quite stupid
He won't chase a ball
But, when he tried to catch one
He jumped into a wall.

He sleeps through the day
And barks in the night
He chases his tail
And he likes to bite.

Despite all his flaws
And how he hates the vets
He makes me laugh
And he's such a good pet.

Peter Baggley (14)
St Joseph's College, Stoke-on-Trent

162

Can You Imagine?

A world with . . .
War
Pain
Suffering
Danger
Discrimination
Hordes of bodies
World poverty?

A world without . . .
War
Pain
Suffering
Danger
Discrimination
Hordes of bodies
World poverty?

Yenu Amarasena (13)
St Joseph's College, Stoke-on-Trent

What Is The War To You?

What is the war to you?
Is it victory or is it death?
Is it to be proud or to be ashamed?
Is it to kill or hide
   Or is it just war?

What is the war to you?
Is it to be a hero or to be a criminal?
Is it to lie down in the mud or to get up and fight?
Is it to wonder what you might have done or to have done it
   Or is it just war?

Through the fields, the red poppies grow
Even through the fighting, hurt and death.

   What is the war to you?

India Wright-Bevans (12)
St Joseph's College, Stoke-on-Trent

163

Love Is . . .

Love is like the sun that never fades.
Love is a colour with lots of different shades.
Love is like summer that always comes back.
Love is a song that becomes your favourite track.
Love is like a special friend hoping that the relationship will never end.
Love is something you always look forward to.
Love is a friendship between me and you.
Love is like chocolate, you want more and more.
Love is a new puppy, you can't help but adore.
Love is like a rubber that erases your mistakes.
Love is like a cake that I love to bake and bake.
Love is like a Heaven, like a romantic weekend down in Devon.
Love is having a special bond.
Love is beautiful, like a decorative pond.

Anna Burgess (13)
St Joseph's College, Stoke-on-Trent

Love Prevails

When war dies
Love prevails
It keeps going strong
Through wind, rain and hail.
The scars of war take time to heal
In love's passionate arms.
I would do anything for you
For your beauty and faith
Even if you're miles away
I'd get to you somehow.
So fly, fly my darling
Into the summer sun
Because I know
When war dies
Love prevails.

Natasha Whetnall (13)
St Joseph's College, Stoke-on-Trent

Where Could It Be?

I looked outside my window,
I looked outside my door.
I looked around the kitchen,
I even looked under the floor.

I looked inside my bed,
Maybe it's all in my head?
Where had it gone?
Where could it be?

How could I have been so stupid?
How could I have been so dumb?
I'd left it in my sock drawer
My mouldy orange plum.

Olivia Commins (14)
St Joseph's College, Stoke-on-Trent

Skiing

Skiing down the mountain
Ever so fast
Having lots of fun
It's such a blast.

Here comes a jump
I'm flying through the air
I'm spinning high and hastily
While spectators stop and stare.

The feeling is amazing
As I travel metres bound
But as I glance downwards
I see I'm about to hit the ground.

Elliot Potts (14)
St Joseph's College, Stoke-on-Trent

The Promises Of War

I see the soldiers
The bombs are like boulders
The soldiers in pain feel cold
Some have things wrong with them, they feel old.

The soldiers are unaware
Of the trap they're walking into.
Some of the soldiers recite the 'Hail Mary'
Some of the dead nearly fall on them.

Men with stretchers sprint
They sprint as fast as they can
A shot goes off behind
It's a good job they ran!

Alex Cartlidge (13)
St Joseph's College, Stoke-on-Trent

I Love You

Love is a flower
Love is a rose
Love is complicated
It comes and goes.

It can last forever
Or just for a day
But if your love's true
Then everything's okay.

It can start with an argument
But end in one too
But there's nothing better than the words
I love you.

Adam Bartley (14)
St Joseph's College, Stoke-on-Trent

Can You Imagine?

Can you imagine
People burning, dying, crying?
Children screaming, hoping, praying,
Helpless.
Can you imagine
Death, decay, bombing?
Bang!
Another dead.
Can you imagine
Hatred, pain, madness,
Choking, choking on
Gas?

Sally Wilbraham (13)
St Joseph's College, Stoke-on-Trent

The War Poem

The sound of screaming filled the air
Now fills the hearts of millions with despair
The sound of guns was all I heard
And the bursting roar of a mechanical bird.
The land was filled with green and red
Most families and friends were already dead
The sight of death disturbed the living
And the rage the enemy's giving.
It was all over in minutes of the day
And all the victors had to say
Was that their deaths are not in vain
But will we go to war again?

Henry Dixon (13)
St Joseph's College, Stoke-on-Trent

Just One

Standing tall in the rain
Engraved upon
The names of some
Who fought for us
And bit the dust
Like the rain, all the same
The ones who loved and cared
And said for king and country
I do declare
I am one of some
Who fought for us
And bit the dust.

Alice Elliott (12)
St Joseph's College, Stoke-on-Trent

Untitled

The sound of an AC130 ahead
Wailing women, children and men in their bed
Chopper gunners hanging low
Which pains the town with sorrow
I can tell nothing will be here tomorrow
Crying and sobbing fills the air
Everywhere to be seen in despair
The attack finishes
Everyone dead
So nothing can be said
The body count is in
Except all the destroyed bodies in the rubble within.

James Hancock (13)
St Joseph's College, Stoke-on-Trent

The Kitchen

Food, lots of it
Staying at my auntie's house
Sweets, chocolates, we are spoilt for choice.

Doughnuts leave sugar round your lips
Crisps, go crunch in my mouth
Sunday dinner, it's like an everlasting gobstopper.

Delicious curry cooking on the hob
Whilst Mum is drowning in smoke
Smoke alarm! Smoke alarm! Mum, are you OK?

Marrium Riaz (14)
St Joseph's College, Stoke-on-Trent

Mankind Must End War Or War Will End Mankind

Dark, dry, deadly heat
Cut, throbbing, bleeding feet.
A flash, a bang
A sudden attack from an Afghan gang
Gunshots, I'm hit.
Two men are dead, help my wounds
With a medical kit.
Bodies dying were once my friends
Now with the Lord their souls we send.

Anthony Colclough (12)
St Joseph's College, Stoke-on-Trent

169

How Precious Is Love?

A garden full of roses, everlasting love.
The sweet smell of romance,
Like diamonds embedded into the earth.
How precious is love?
The eyes of passion and romance,
Flickers like a candle,
A scene like the sunset,
Like the touch of her gentle lips,
How precious is love?

Imogen Storer (13)
St Joseph's College, Stoke-on-Trent

Champions

1966 World Cup final at Wembley
England playing favourites, tag team, West Germany
Geoff Hurst the hero, scoring us 3
England win 4-2, the trophy is free

44 years later
We want it again
So let's go to Africa
And win it in 2010!

Harry McKirdy (12)
St Joseph's College, Stoke-on-Trent

Love!

Love is forever, never does it deem
We're stuck together, we'll never cry,
Love is a heart broken in two
It goes back together with the love for you.

You make me happy, we smile, we love.
You make me tingle but just after that we're sadly single.

Devon Martin (12)
St Joseph's College, Stoke-on-Trent

Holocaust

Can you imagine the pain and suffering
Of those brave men that fought for us?
Dying, choking, drowning in gas,
Helpless, what can I do?

Before my very eyes they fall
One by one they disappear.
My friends, my pals, for them it's too late
And all I can think is, is it me next?

Francesca Short (13)
St Joseph's College, Stoke-on-Trent

Wear Your Poppy With Pride

When you hear your money rattle
Think of those who fought in battle.
To help the injured and the lame
Do your best to remember their name.
They died for us so we could be free
Fighting in battle, land, air and sea.
Up into Heaven on angel wings they ride
We will remember them - wear your poppy with pride!

Katie Ratcliffe (13)
St Joseph's College, Stoke-on-Trent

My Little Nelly

My little Nelly, what can I say?
She's as mad as a hatter
And just loves to play!
Pitter-patter, pitter-patter
The sound of her paws
All mucky and wet
She slides across floors
My little Nelly, my favourite pet.

Claire Austerberry (13)
St Joseph's College, Stoke-on-Trent

171

Lovebirds' Song

Love is like a summer's day.
It keeps you warm and snug always.
It clutches you with happiness
So you will never cry with sadness.
It spins you round in an everlasting flow
Full of love and a romantic blow.
So here we are, let the lovebirds fly
In the sky, so high, so high.

Chantelle Hough (13)
St Joseph's College, Stoke-on-Trent

The Gas

So many men, I see them all go down
Crying and screaming, death will be upon them soon
I see them drowning in a sea of green
Their faces turning from green to red to blue
Choking up their guts and blood
I feel so helpless watching them die
And I start to moan as though I'm in there with them
Oh when will this terror end?

Alisha Afzal (13)
St Joseph's College, Stoke-on-Trent

Memorial

M en dying everywhere
E verywhere the dead like sleeping
M en perished where tortured
O verpowered by the Nazis
R emember this day for years to come
I magine you were in that position
A bsolutely devastating!
L ots of people will be thought of in their minds.

Matthew Nixon (12)
St Joseph's College, Stoke-on-Trent

Can You Imagine?

Can you imagine a world without war?
A world with peace and no more guns.
If that was the case it'd be the end of torture, bombs and
discrimination.
Also there would be fewer problems for our nation.
There would be fewer deaths, devastation and destroyed places
At last we wouldn't see so many sad faces.

Just think, fighting solves nothing,
All it does is cause the loss of our soldiers . . . and their families
crying.
In this modern day there should be more options
Without causing so much corruption.

Nowadays war should not happen.
It should just be a thing in the past which has been forgotten.
We will always remember our loyal soldiers
But let's hope war has come . . . and gone!

George Bradbury (12)
St Joseph's College, Stoke-on-Trent

The Seven Ages Of Man
(Inspired by 'As You Like It' by Shakespeare)

'All the world's a stage
And all the men and women merely players
They have their exits and their entrances'
And one bag in its time having many parts
Its acts being seven stages. At first the school bag
Messy and holding the owner's books.
Then the make-up bag with the mirror,
And a flashy mobile phone, silver like stars,
Unwanted for practicality. And the suitcase,
Moving to new places with a fresh future,
Exploring possibilities widely. Then the laptop case,
Full of information, under computer's desk.
Wanting to be from Harrods, not the market,
Looking for high popularity,
Even when there's pressure. And the nappy bags,
In soft cotton tied around the baby's bum.
With gentle edges and in constant use,
Full of soft fabrics and baby stories,
So it's used again. The sixth age shifts
Into a black leather handbag
With various shopping trips and a full purse
For its silky leather and its velvety inside,
Turning into hard, flaky material
And dog-eared edges. The last scene of all
That ends strange, eventful history,
A tartan trolley bag and a walking aid,
No style, no luck, no money, just a bag full of peppermint sweets.

Alice Cottam (13)
Windsor Park Middle School, Uttoxeter

Sonnet

Two classrooms quite unlike in atmosphere,
In our school building (where I write this down),
One teacher smiles and jumps around and cheers,
The other seems to stare and shout and frown.
A set of children whisper and laugh loud,
Whilst from their neighbours there's a silent hush,
Test results leave one set of children proud,
Much more successful than the bunch who rush.
Lunchtime is such a mix of friends and foes,
Each corner of the playground has its cliques,
Discussing fashion, boys and trendy clothes,
The boys are acting cool and showing tricks.
School life with all its ups and downs is fine,
Those fleeting years are such a special time.

Lily Hassall (13)
Windsor Park Middle School, Uttoxeter

First Love

When this class is over, I must tell her
I saw her on the playground, years ago
Since then, her heart, I just want to conquer
When should I tell her? I just do not know . . .
I'm filled with great fear, what if I'm too late?
What if her heart belongs to another?
I wish for her to want to be soulmates
Fear creeps; will she want me as a love?
No! I tell myself it's now or never!
I look at the clock, time seems to have slowed
I need to say how I've felt forever
If I don't I'm just going to explode.
My heart is beating, my dreams have come true
And from that moment on, our love just grew.

Sam Haywood (13)
Windsor Park Middle School, Uttoxeter

The Seven Ages Of Man
(Inspired by 'As You Like It' by Shakespeare)

And all the men and women are just contestants
And one person participates in many different things in their life.
He goes through seven stages. At first the wannabe,
Screaming and shouting at the voice of a celebrity.
Then the auditionee creeping into the spotlight
Willingly to fame. And then the competitor,
Winning the love of teenagers everywhere.
They watch his every step. Then the finalist,
Hair gelled back and a cheeky grin on his face,
Jealous of the other competitors but confident himself,
So close to all the fame.
Even at the bleakest moment. Then the No 1 hit artist,
He is best friends with the people he once dreamed about,
Full of money he goes for the ultimate goal. The sixth age moves,
To a world mega star, everyone knows his name,
Somehow his cheeky smile has become more solemn now.
All he cares about now is money, his old friends he long since left.
His once good looks have been smothered in orange spray tan.
He is more blank, his emotion is faked to him, this is the tip of his career.
He is now a has-been, one for the grannies, his real career has ended.
His soft brown hair has changed one too many times as the grey appears,
No looks, no screaming fans, no real joy, nothing.

Hannah Clemett (13)
Windsor Park Middle School, Uttoxeter

The Seven Ages Of Man

(Inspired by 'As You Like it' by Shakespeare)

Life is a merry-go-round
It goes round and round with its ups and downs
Until it finally stops.
On our journey through life we ride it seven times.
The first is the crawling baby going round and round in his playpen,
Gurgling with delight.
The moaning teenager zooming round on his board with wheels,
Without a care.
And then the yobbo, who gets his kicks by hotwiring cars, cruising round
Whilst smoking spliffs.
Then comes the time to settle down with that special someone,
Getting hitched and placing the band of gold on her finger.
And then middle age sets in, the wife, the kids, work and money,
'Want, want, want' then 'Gimme, gimme, gimme.'
'Lie down, get up' work and money all the time.
The sixth ride, retired with our bus passes in our hands,
Takes us to the garden centres, potted plants and OAP lunches.
Zimmer frames at the ready, stumbling round,
With our dodgy hips, if you're lucky avoiding the trips.
Then the final ride, wheeled around the care home in a wheelchair,
Without a care, not knowing a thing.
Sitting there snoozing and rambling on
Until life comes to an end.

Lewis Leadbetter (13)
Windsor Park Middle School, Uttoxeter

White Horses

Below me, the tide is washing them away
Below me, the waves are swaying their manes
Below me, the children play in their territory
Above me, the sky, broken by candyfloss clouds

Below me, my distraught mother, crying in a corner
Below me, my weeping father, saddened and alone
Below me, my family in pieces and helplessly hysterical
Above me, the glowing, calling my name

Below me, boats circle the scene of disruption
Below me, the people search for the rotting corpse
Below me, they are giving up all hope
Above me, I see the light of eternity

Below me, I have left behind my life
Below me, I have left behind my body
Below me, I have left without a single goodbye
Above me, my next stop in life

Me, I'm dead
Me, I'm going to Heaven
Me, I drowned
Me, I was killed by white horses.

Myles Verdon (12)
Windsor Park Middle School, Uttoxeter

Can We Stop It Now? - Haiku

Gas, bangs, death, hatred.
World is being torn apart,
Can we stop it now?

Jarrad Lambie (13)
Wood Green High School, Wednesbury

Have You Ever Felt The Feeling Of Intensity?

Have you ever felt the feeling of intensity?
Something so hard to escape
Have you ever felt the division it creates
From the rest of the world?

Did you ever wonder why emotion was so hard,
So binding and blinding, it cuts to the heart?
Did you ever witness the loss of emotion,
How it succeeded to stop all motion?

Have you ever felt love so strong
It blinds you and binds you until someone breaks the song?
Have you ever felt a broken heart
When it jolts and falters as it tries to restart?

Did you ever feel hatred so strong
It binds you and blinds you until you realise you were wrong?
Did you ever find out why you were so sad,
Was it that deep hatred that made you feel bad?
Have you ever missed the sense of purity
When your home's gone, no security?
Have you felt inner blindness
Where all sense is cut off; replaced with no kindness?

Have you ever felt the feeling of intensity?
Something so hard to escape.
Have you ever felt the division it creates
Of love, hatred and the world?

Waseelah Smedley (13)
Wood Green High School, Wednesbury

Unrequited Love

A venomous speech falls from your lips, fed to me as chocolate
would a child.
Slaughtering my hope, murdering my belief.
This dense cloud of sadness and anger,
This burden that won't fade.
My strong love, my intense hate,
My incomplete mind,
Internal organs, shutting down with every step I take.
The fingers of my dying heart
Stretch and grasp,
Intertwined, trapped.
The heavenly scent and angelic complexion,
Engraving themselves into my memory,
Haunting.
I blossom like a white rose in full bloom when we meet,
At the height of summer, the dispersion of the sun's rays.
When I catch a glimpse of your sparkling eyes,
Happiness, freedom.
Freedom from the conflict,
Broken world, broken heart.
Freedom from this pain I feel,
This devouring world we inhabit,
This blackening soul, forever rotting within,
Eternally dead, without you.

Molly Ashfield-Hayes (13)
Wood Green High School, Wednesbury

I Love You With All My Heart

I love you with all my heart
But you don't understand
That when I say hello to you
I can barely stand.

You are the smiling sun
That beams a thousand rays
You are as bright as a firecracker
I dream about those days.

Your laughter is my world
That circles me with joy
You make me so satisfied
Like a new toy.

Your warm and humble tone
Reminds me of the sun
You cover me with happiness
It feels like I have won.

But when I say goodbye to you
You still don't understand
I love you with all my heart
Please give me your hand.

Sharnpreet Kaur Cheema (12)
Wood Green High School, Wednesbury

Darkness

Darkness is as dark as dark can be,
It fills us with despair and grief.
It kills hope with anger, a black sea,
Crippling, aging, a blackened leaf.

Time and time again, going around the bend
Losing everything in life
And from the deep, dark blackness, it descends,
This deep, black abyss, a sweeping knife.

This being now stumbling in the dark
A blind old man weeping with despair.
An old cave reading, an ancient mark,
Comes this tale of a black grizzly bear.

In the air with a sense of depression
A poison to the mind, black,
Never lifting, a dense sense of tension,
Ultimately breaking one's back.

So this is how it destroys us now,
A new sense of feeble longing,
Through the deathly darkness does it prowl
Waiting, claiming souls, unbelonging.

Ahmed Hans (13)
Wood Green High School, Wednesbury

Surrounded

As the barbed wire surrounded us
We were separated
She went to get the bus
I finally mated!

I was alone in the dark
It sounded like a storm over the sea
I could get through, that one arc
But, that noise, what could it be?

Soldiers killing time after time
People losing others
We were committing crimes
It was mostly their mothers

That barbed wire that surrounded me
No education, or transport
It devastated my fantasy
I really think we should have been taught!

Nicky Cavell (12)
Wood Green High School, Wednesbury

Segregation

Surrounded in fear, no way out
Segregation
Covered in cowardice, no existence
Segregation
Claustrophobic, no emotion
Segregation
Hiding, no escape
Segregation
Loneliness, never-ending
Segregation
Lonely, but never more
Segregation.

David Young (13)
Wood Green High School, Wednesbury

183

Intensity

I heard it, it was after me,
I had the sudden surge of intensity.
The longer I walked, the darker it became
The sky was decorated by showers of rain.

The wind howled through the sky,
Thunder and lightning were close nearby.
The moon was a pure white pearl
Branches of trees became curled.

I heard footsteps behind me which gave me a fright
This will teach you not to go to the woods at night.
I ran without taking any care
I was a hawk stalking its prey in the air.

I fell onto the dark misty floor,
I was to be seen no more.

Josh Southall (13)
Wood Green High School, Wednesbury

I Love You

Every time I see those sky-blue eyes
They send my heart a-racing
Your eyes are like those star-cluttered skies
Brimming with beauty, mystery and love
My heart longs for you, my head tells me lies
It tries to tell me you'll never be the one
But I hope our love will never meet its demise.
Every time you glance at me
I hear the Heaven bells a-ringing
As if God has rung for His dearest angel
Even for you nature starts singing
My beauty, my love, my eternal soulmate
The warmth to my heart you keep bringing
I love you but do you love me?

Leanne Stanfield (13)
Wood Green High School, Wednesbury

Young Writers Information

We hope you have enjoyed reading this book - and that you will continue to enjoy it in the coming years.

If you like reading and writing poetry drop us a line, or give us a call, and we'll send you a free information pack.

Alternatively if you would like to order further copies of this book or any of our other titles, then please give us a call or log onto our website at www.youngwriters.co.uk.

Young Writers Information
Remus House
Coltsfoot Drive
Peterborough
PE2 9JX
(01733) 890066